THE SPORADIC THOUGHTS OF A BLACK BROOKLYN INTELLECT

The Sporadic Thoughts Of A Black Brooklyn Intellect

GENCIANO VITO CLOTTER

Junior's Promise Publishing

Copyright © 2020 by Genciano Clotter and Juniors Promise LLC

All rights reserved. No part of this book may be reproduced in any form or by any electronic or mechanical means, including information storage and retrieval systems, without permission in writing from the author, except by reviewer, who may quote brief passages in a review. Scanning, uploading, recording and electronic distribution of this book or the facilitation of such without the permission of the author is strictly prohibited.

Book Cover design by Falola Akinlana
Instagram: @ojotats

Editor: Reishon Cordero
Instagram: @staxxcordero

Dedicated to Brooklyn

(Spread Love It's the Brooklyn Way
Notorious B.I.G.)

1

Let's Get the Proceedings, Proceeding This Evening

The Completely Sporadic Thoughts of a Black Brooklyn Intellect

Jay-Z is my favorite rapper of all times (no typo)! This is not because of the millions of albums he has sold, his great business acumen, or his phenomenal lyricism; Shawn Jay-Z Carter is my favorite rapper of all times because of what he symbolizes in my life. Growing up as a poor black boy from Bed-Stuy Brooklyn, it was hard for me to see how I was going to make it out of my neighborhood. There is this kinda strange thing that happens to black boys when they enter high school. It seems like society view us all as criminals. Its as if our rite of passage as teenagers is the criminalization of our black bodies. So, the same police officers who would wave hi to us and comfort us by their presence when we were younger now view us with scorn and treat us like suspects. Parents who we had great relationships with now can't understand us and blame us for a society that you barely had time to impact. Gang members either want to recruit us or hurt us. All the while we are just trying to figure out who you are and what we want to be in life.

    I was no different. I felt the difference in how I was viewed and treated when I became a high school freshman. I was scared of the bloods in my neighborhood because I heard they would ask you for the time and then cut your face (a buck 50 for those who need to know the slang term.) Police officers treat and view me as if I had no rights. I can't tell you how many times I would be hanging out in front of my building just for undercover cops to approach me in a manner that made me think I was being robbed, frisk me for no reason and leave without even an explanation as to why the approached me. You add the facts that my dad died when I was 8, my mom's new husband hating us, (which was fine because the feeling was mutual) and a completely normal identity crisis; and I had no idea how I was gonna make it out of the hood. Either the gangs, police, dysfunctional family or fatigue was gonna get me.

But in the midst of all this I had Reasonable Doubt (all pun intended!) An album that would take me more than 15 years, 12 movies, and a multitude of life experiences to understand. It became one of the many soundtracks of my life. Songs like *Politics as Usual* and *Dead Presidents* touched my soul way before I even knew what their lyrics meant. As I continued to listen to the album

The Completely Sporadic Thoughts of a Black Brooklyn Intellect

I began to understand the metaphors and similes woven masterfully throughout the project. I literally grew up with the album being able to refer back to it and relate to different situations as I lived through them. The song *Can I Live* encompassed many of my struggles as well as a question that would later turn into my proclamation. Can I Live? Nah Can I Live! (As in you need to chill and give me some space so I can do me.)

I bought all of Jay-Z's other albums he had out at the time (I bought Reasonable Doubt in 1998) and found out we were both born in the same Hospital (Woodhull Hospital). He also lived in Marcy Projects where I used to frequent because my Auntie Nena lived there (My cousins had Super Nintendo and I didn't so it was a paradise over there minus the gun shots). But the most important thing Jay-Z ever did for me was make it out the hood! Shawn Carter was physical proof that you could make it out the hood. And shit if a man that was born in the same place and grew up in the same neighborhood as me made it out, then that means I could make it out too! Jay-Z figuratively and literally gave me reason to doubt who society said I was as a black boy and what society said I could achieve. For that Jay-Z will always be the greatest!

The connection I have to Jay-Z was only possible because Shawn Carter decided to write rhymes. There is something inherently powerful about documenting your story. Whether it is a diary, a letter, a song, a poem or a screenplay, documenting creates a form of immortality so much so that you can have a conversation with, be challenged by or even argue with someone who has been dead for years. You can also do those things with people you have never met. This creates the opportunity for you to be inspired, be moved by, and find hope in someone you don't even know. I have had the honor of symbolically sitting at the feet of James Baldwin, have been called into action by Malcolm X, been hugged and healed by bell hooks, and debated the decisions of Martin Luther all because of their writings. Movies and songs have a similar effect in that they can move and inspire with no expiration date. All this stems from people who sat down one day and decided to document something when they were inspired.

The Completely Sporadic Thoughts of a Black Brooklyn Intellect

A classmate once told me God gives you a sermon (message) everyday, the question is are you paying attention. I feel God talks to us everyday through experiences, songs, family members, conversations etc. God deposits brilliance into us through these mediums and when we document that brilliance, when we document our interactions, a part of us is eternalized. The words you wrote at 2am in the morning from a heartbreak can be used to heal a teenager trying to figure it all out 10 years later on the same day as your wedding. God is talking to us everyday, the question is are we listening?

Whether you believe in God, Allah, the ancestors, the universe or just people, when you share your desires and dreams, I believe there is a response. Whether you share them in the form of prayer, writings, affirmations or conversations, some of the things we desire most in life are given to us in the form of intangible thoughts. The financial freedom that you are praying for, the job you have been searching for and the purpose that you have been looking for can all be requests answered by an idea that randomly pops in your head. The question is what are you going to do with that great idea when it pops in your head? Are you going to take the time to cultivate those intangible thoughts into something more or will you waste that anointing? Some of us are in the situations we are in not because our prayers weren't answered but because we are doing nothing even though our prayers were.

If you are opening this book, first let me say thank you! This book is my attempt to share my thoughts in an effort to positively impact the world. Like Reasonable Doubt, I pray that the impact of this book will last beyond my lifetime and inspire folks way after I'm gone. This is my version of Reasonable Doubt. This is also me being responsive to the inspiration that was given to me. If you have been inspired to do something (write a screenplay, shoot a movie, write a book, make an album, start a business, etc.,) put this book down and start doing it! The positive change in your life will depend on how you use the inspired intangible thoughts you have in your head. So before you proceed with this book, proceed with your inspiration. Just remember to come back to the book lol. Not only will it change your life but it may change someone else's as well.

Jay-Z made me reasonably doubt that my life was destined for failure no matter what I did. I have become a better man because of bell hooks. I learned to be audacious and love myself because of Malcolm X and I learned to challenge my faith because of James Baldwin. The following pages are some of the revelations God has shared with me. These are sporadic thoughts I have about a multitude of topics. Feel free to argue, disagree, and converse with me along the way. But if you have something to start, if you have a Reasonable Doubt you need to make, make it! If you have proceedings you need to proceed with, please do so. There are lives that depend on it. My name is Genciano Clotter. My friends call me Vito and with that being said….

Let's Get the Proceedings, Proceeding this evening!!

2

Wasn't Posed to Make it Past 25

The Completely Sporadic Thoughts of a Black Brooklyn Intellect

When I woke up on my 18th birthday I cried for about 5 minutes. Honestly, I never thought I was going to make it to 18 (refer back to chapter one for the reasons lol). Turns out the Bloods in my neighborhood ended up being family. However, there was still the issues of being raised in a broken home, living in a violent pre gentrified Brooklyn and not knowing if you were going to be shot by other crews or police. So 18 was an unbelievable gift from God to me.

I recently taught at a high school for a year. It was the worst place I have ever worked in my life. I had a choice of teaching at a plethora of schools but I chose to teach at a school that was in my old neighborhood. There was no other place I would have rather taught than Bed-Stuy, Brooklyn. I wanted to return home and share all the knowledge I had acquired since I had left to go to Princeton Theological Seminary. What was mindboggling to me was my academic success alienated me from both the students and the teachers. The teachers (of which none of whom were black or

EVER LIVED IN BED-STUY) told me that I had to understand the conditions that these kids came from as if I wasn't raised in the same neighborhood. I was a co-teacher but had to cover classes without lesson plans from teachers who were absent way too much and cared more about their job security than actually teaching the kids. So, when I came into the classroom with high expectations for my students they quickly rejected me not because they couldn't do the work, but because they weren't required to do that much normally. Regardless of this friction I tried to teach my students not just school lessons but life lessons. After all, they weren't just my students; they were my neighbors, my relatives, and my people! I didn't drive out the neighborhood after school; I lived there and had a stake in their success beyond their grades.

Joking on teachers is commonplace in high school. Some of my students would joke on me because I was balding and was growing grey hair. This was hilarious to me considering the fact that if God spared life (shout out to the West- Indian massive) they too will have the privilege of getting older and honestly I never thought I would be this age. Seeing my body change and evolve with time has been a blessing to someone who never thought he would make it to 34.

Kanye West released his first album College Dropout in 2004. On this classic album there is a song entitled *We don't care*. The line that moves me the most in this song is, "We weren't supposed to make it past 25, jokes on you we still alive". There is nothing logically that says I should be where I am. My father (deceased) migrated here from Honduras with no more than a junior high school education. My mother didn't get her G.E.D. until she was well into her 40s. I'm an Afro-Latino Garifuna cultured black man from the hood. I never thought I would grow up to graduate from college and obtain two masters degrees. These accomplishments are so beyond any dream that I ever had for myself that I really feel that I'm living a bonus life. But since I was given reasonable doubt about the how society viewed me I guess I always knew there was a chance. I wasn't supposed to make it past 25 but jokes on them, I'm still alive.

Not believing that I would make it past 25 has had an interesting impact on my life. Believing I would die young stunted the goals I had for myself. I have over achieved in my 34 years of life so now I have to create new goals for myself. Goals that I want my students and children to have as teens. Not believing I would make it to 25 also impacted how I loved others and myself. When society tells you that your life has no value you sometimes believe it. It has taken years for me to recover from the trauma of being a black boy in America.

However, not feeling I had a place in this society allowed me to critique social norms and reject common views held by society. It has also allowed me to empathize with others who have been pushed to the margins. My life has become a testament to the fact that the stigmas that are associated with society's norms are false. Many of these norms hinder the growth of all of us and allow many of us to live in ignorance. When I realized society was wrong about me, I stopped listening to what society had to say about everyone else. I will never leave the responsibility of defining who

I am and what I am capable of, in such undeserving hands again. In the great words of Jay-Z when people start trying to limit you have to "Remind yourself, nobody built like you, you designed yourself." (Dream- Jay-Z Blue Print II). Don't ever give anyone, any institution, any country, or any group the responsibility of defining you! Use the doubt people have of you as motivation to fuel your dreams. Society is filled with people who have no idea how God, Allah, the ancestors, and the universe have crafted you. They also don't know that world changing intangible thought that you are about to manifest. They just looked at you and doubt you…

Whelp….

> We wasn't supposed to make past 25
>
> Jokes on you we still alive
>
> Throw your hands up into the sky
>
> And say we don't care what people say
>
> Kanye West – We Don't Care- College Drop Out

3

Around My Block

The Completely Sporadic Thoughts of a Black Brooklyn Intellect

When you grow up in the hood you notice the people who get the most attention. You notice the love and admiration they get because of the money they have, the cars they drive, the clothes they wear, the crimes they commit and the people they date. Inevitably you begin to want that attention, love and admiration yourself so being that person becomes your goal. Like them, you too aspire to reach the top of the hood social construct. You want to be the Woman or Man on the block! You want to be the person that, when you come outside, everyone stops what they're doing and runs to you showing you reverence. So the block becomes the world to you. No other place has more bearing on how you are viewed and how you value yourself than the block. You can be popular in school but if you hold no social standing on the block you aren't really popular. At the end of the day nothing matters more than the block so in your mind the block is your world. You acquire a block mentality. There of course is a major flaw in this mindset however. One begins to think that the whole world exists in a 5-block radius. Outside of going shopping, going to school or working, every other aspect of your life revolves around the same structures and people. This makes you close to everyone in your hood but it also limits your vision as to what life is and ultimately what life can truly offer.

I used to work at Cold Stone Creamery on Time Square for a few years (Top 5 hired or fired... Platinum Doh!). During that time, some friends that I met in High School invited me to go to Cancun. I heard about Cancun but never really cared to venture outside of my neighborhood. I asked my close friends if they wanted to come along with me and they agreed, so we all went on the trip. To get there I had to work 50-60 hours a week for a few weeks. As we got closer to the trip, I would receive updates on where we were going to stay and the things we were going to do while we were there. I was shown pictures of the villa we booked and was told about the parties we were attending but I didn't really believe it because I'm from the hood; most of the time when things seem too good to be true they normally are. I got on the plane and when I landed in

Cancun I was blown away. Immediately my whole mindset about my block and its importance changed!

When I got to Cancun, I noticed that the water was clear unlike the green water back home in New York. Food was relatively cheap and so were the drinks (shout out to happy hour at the pool bar). My friends and I had a great time and I left Cancun with one thing on my mind. What was the point of being popular on the block? There was absolutely no clear water there, or fun parties (well not like Cancun) so why did I feel I had an obligation to the block? Why did I hold that social construct in a higher regard than any other? Why was the block my world? My Cancun trip taught me that not only was there life off my block but there was life more abundantly.

As I began to try and acquire enough stamps in my passport to mess with young H.O. (Jay-Z reference), I began to see that there was great variety in how different countries functioned. As Americans, we are taught that we are the greatest country in the world with the smartest people. But a simple Google search will inform us that Canada contains the most people with education after high school. On that list we aren't 2nd, 3rd or even 4th. We are 6th in the world. We also boast that we are the land of the free while simultaneously incarcerating our citizens at a higher rate than any other country in the world. We literally average a mass shooting everyday and are told that we need to keep the right to bear arms while Police officers in London don't even carry guns. As I travelled around the world, I began to think maybe other countries are doing things that we can learn from. I slowly began to realize that just like I had a block mentality that kept me on my block thinking that it was the totality of life, many Americans have a block mentality in that we believe that the United States is the best functioning country in the world when that is far from the truth. I love the United States but my travel and reading has shown me that not only are other countries functioning better than we are in important areas, but if we want to improve as a country, we really should learn from them.

The Completely Sporadic Thoughts of a Black Brooklyn Intellect

I recently went to London to celebrate their Caribbean carnival. While I was there I spoke with some locals about crime. They shared with me that they have a problem with stabbings that happen quite frequently throughout the city. I responded by saying, they are lucky that is their only problem. People get shot all the time in the United States. While we average a mass shooting a day and have issues with over-militarized police, their police officers don't even carry guns. At a carnival where well over a million people were out in the street, officers were able to maintain the safety of both citizens and tourists without having to have a gun around their waist. That made me question, Do we really need guns for safety if London doesn't? Or were we conditioned to believe that the only way we can be safe is if someone has a gun? Is this our Americanized block mentality?

I know I have already stated it twice before, but WE AVERAGE ONE MASS SHOOTING a day in this country. Mass shootings happen so often that its hard not to be desensitized to them. There seems to be no way for us to stop mass shootings. BUT... there is a country that had this problem and solved it. That country is Australia. In 1996 Martin Bryant opened fire and killed 35 people and wounded 18 others in Port Arthur Australia. Within weeks Australia banned semi-automatic weapons and other military-style weapons. Since then, there hasn't been any mass shootings in Australia! Imagine how many lives would had been saved if after the Columbine High School tragedy the United States Congress would had done the same thing. There is something we could learn from both London and Australia about the necessity of guns. Our belief in guns stems from our own block mentality but other countries have a better handle on safety than we do.

 We also incarcerate more of our own citizens than any other country in the world by a very large margin. Instead of the land of the free we should be called the land of the incarcerated. Our Criminal Justice system is broken. It's more accurately more of a criminal retention system than a justice system. There are individuals in jail because they committed crimes but also others who are there because they can't pay bail, and because they were pressured to plead guilty to crimes they didn't commit. Ideally, jail is supposed to rehabilitate criminals and help them become better members of society. However, many come out suffering from the trauma they endured while being locked up. Others go in and become better criminals. This system doesn't help criminals' reform; it helps criminals repeat their crimes. Not only that, if you are convicted of a crime you didn't commit, you may come into the system innocent and leave a criminal. 70% of persons who are freed from jail in the United States are re-arrested within 5 years. This claim in not an indictment on lawyers, judges, or others who work for the system; its an indictment on the system itself. When we think about the criminal justice system, it's hard to think of a way to stop the many ills that plague it. Our block mentality has shortened our sight to what can yet be done. But if you are looking for a country that is already doing something we haven't been able to do yet. You need only look at the country of Norway.

Norway has the least amount of repeat offenders percentage wise in the world. Only 20% of freed persons in Norway are re-arrested. Norway also has one of the lowest crime rates and one of the most humane prison systems in the world as well. The accommodations for prisoners are nice and they have vocational programs to help prisoners land jobs when they leave. The punishment for prisoners is the act of taking their freedom away. In Norway inmates are treated well. Inmates and guards have great relationships. Norway believes in restorative justice, which focuses on helping the inmate and not punishing and dehumanizing them. Imagine what the United States could be if we restored our inmates like Norway and not cage them and treat them like animals. Imagine what the United States could be if we passed common sense gun laws after mass shootings like Australia or demilitarized our police officers like London. My world travel took the blinders off my eyes and allowed me to see that there is a better way to live life than the way I lived it on my block. My travel also showed me that there is a better way to live life than the way we have been doing it in this country. Traveling helps change your perspective on life. It allows you to critically think about your living conditions and what you believe is important. When I stayed on my block I believed that way of life was the best way of life until I saw something different. As an American, I believed the way we did things were the most optimal until I went to other countries. There is so much we can learn from other countries. Many of them have solved the problems we are currently struggling with. In order for us to truly be great, America we need to get rid of our block mentality!

4

We Hold These Truths

The Declaration of independence is basically a break up letter between the 13 colonies and Great Britain. This Declaration explains why the 13 colonies were going to sever ties with their parent country and form a country of their own. The Declaration of Independence is a powerful document on which many of our American ideals stand. After a brief introduction as to the purpose of the document we receive these words:

> *We hold these truths to be self-evident, that all men are created equal, that they are endowed by their Creator with certain unalienable Rights, that among these are Life, Liberty and the pursuit of Happiness.*

Politicians and patriotic Americans alike boasting of the greatness of this country utter these words with pride. However, if we were to examine this text and mirror it against the history of America, we would see that not only is America falling short of this ideal,

America has never lived up to the promises found in this document.

   Before we comb over this text, lets define three words so we all are on the same page. The term self-evident means: not needed to be explained or obvious. Its like DUH everyone knows that! The next term is Unalienable rights. This term means: rights that cannot be taken away or given away. The last word is endowed. Endowed means: given or provided by. Knowing these terms we can now paraphrase this document by writing:

> *We hold these truths to be obvious, all people were created equal, people are given rights by God that they can't give away nor can any human take away. Among these rights (but not limited to) are the right to life, liberty and the pursuit of happiness.*

   These are the obvious truths of America. We are all equal and we all have rights that can't be given away or taken away. The only problem is America has never lived up to these words. It's almost as if America caught amnesia after the words *we hold these truths* because never in her history has all persons in this country been equal. While the ink on this document was drying there were slaves serving the very men who wrote it. The Native Americans who graciously helped the first pilgrims survive this new world were mutilated and villainized in an effort to take their land. Africans were enslaved and were forced to work in this country for no pay. When Italians and Germans came to this country they faced racism from "whites" that felt they weren't American enough. When John F. Kennedy ran for President, the fact that he was a Roman Catholic was an issue with Americans. I still haven't mentioned Jim Crow, Civil Rights, women's rights, LGBTQIA+ rights, the Japanese-Americans who had to live in camps during World War 2 solely because of their heritage, Latin American rights or the rights of the disabled. It took legislation in early 2019 for black women to legally be able to wear their natural hair to work. When in our history has the equal rights among men and been women obvious? When has it been equal for whites and minorities? From the origin of this institution, equality hasn't been given, it has been something many of us had to fight and die for. Simultaneously, others of us who benefit from this lack of equality passively encourage those of us who don't share in such privileges to be patient. However, if the right of equality was self-evident, why do we have to wait? There is nothing in the Declaration that says this right of equality would come after a while or someday. It clearly states that we are equal at birth so why should some of us receive the birthright of equality while others are asked to wait?

If we have born with unalienable rights, why wasn't the slave born in America given the same rights as the slave owner? Why wasn't the Black Sergeant that fought for this country given the same privileges as the white private who came home? It seems to me that after the words we hold these truths, no other part of the Declaration of Independence was ever actualized. This is not to suggest that America is a horrible country. This however is to underscore the fact that America has never lived up to whom he said he is on paper. America has killed the black and brown woman and man for pursuing their dreams. America has taken away the unalienable rights that the Declaration of Independence clearly states is not in their jurisdiction to take away.

America is a land of inequality, which can clearly be seen by the way women and men are paid differently for the same job. What America has certainly done though that is documented in the Declaration of Independence is hold truths. They hold the truth that Blacks in this country have to fight for every unalienable right their white counterparts is birth with. They hold the truth that same sex couples are still not given the same liberties that heterosexual couples abuse. They hold the truth that women still don't get paid the same as men even when they do the same job. America is holding the truth from us and instead, America points back to empty words from a document that has never been actualized. It would be different if the forefathers of this country wrote we hold these truths to be self-evident that someday all men will be created equal but that is not what is written. We were all equal in 1776 supposedly. But the day of equality, of life, liberty and happiness for all has still not come.

As a country we need to no longer hold these truths but live these truths. This requires that those of us who receive these rights fight for those of us who don't instead of asking them for patience. We are better than what we currently are as a country and we need to do better to be what we said we were all those years ago. Until we do, we are stilling hold these truths and living in denial.

5

Whiteness is a Mental Disease

Have you ever looked up the traits of a sociopath?
Some of the traits include the following:

- Inadequately motivated antisocial behavior
- Superficial charm and good intelligence
- Unreliability
- Untruthfulness and insincerity
- Lack of remorse and shame
- Poor judgment and failure to learn by experience

It is important to define terms to ensure there is a meeting of the minds (that we are talking about the same thing or at the very least you understand what I'm talking about.) When I refer to the word "whiteness," I'm NOT talking about Caucasians in so much that I'm talking about individuals who do not identify with their historical land of origin. So the first part of my definition of whiteness is an individual who erases their history and does not use a hyphen. By hyphen I mean someone who doesn't identify as being Italian- American or German-American etc. This is important because no matter how many generations you are removed from your family's migration to the United States (or colonies) this hyphen underscores the universal and fundamental fact that you are NOT the original people of this country. The hyphen shows that just like African Americans and Asian Americans we all came from somewhere else. This hyphen not only gives respect to Native Americans who are the original people of this land but it is also what makes this country great. The hyphen shows that people from all over the world came to America and the greatness of this country comes from the global collaborations and contributes of this global collective. The absence of this hyphen or lack of acknowledgement of one's history before coming to United States may lead to the incorrect belief that you are the original people of this land. This is the first attribute to the mental disease, which is whiteness.

The second attribute to the mental disease called whiteness is a complete disregard to history. This can be correlated with the sociopathic traits of untruthfulness and insincerity as well as poor judgment and failure to learn from experiences. We have seen these traits in whites that make the statement "lift yourself up by your own bootstraps." How is this statement a sign of the mental disease of whiteness? Well it begins with the holiday of Thanksgiving. Thanksgiving commemorates the act of kindness Native Americans showed migrating Pilgrims when they reached this land. Natives taught the Pilgrims how to plant corn, fish and hunt amongst other things. Without the kindness of Native Americans, Pilgrims would not have survived this new world. This is not at all lifting themselves up by their own bootstraps. From the inception of what we now call the United States of America, progress occurred because folks helped one another and not because people did things by themselves. Sadly, the Pilgrims came across the Atlantic Ocean with small pokes, yellow fever, cholera, typhus and the plague, which devastated the Native population. The Pilgrims who landed on the shores of America sick and in need of help would soon lead a genocidal campaign called manifest destiny to take over the land the Natives freely shared with them (If you want to find a dope song about this check out Lupe Fiasco's Unforgivable Youth.) During this campaign Natives were no longer considered the friendly companions who helped the sick and lowly Pilgrims survive this new world. They were villianized and painted as savages in order that the theft and pillaging of their land can take place. This action can be attributed to the sociopathic trait of inadequately motivated antisocial behavior.

Antisocial behavior can be interpreted as being unwilling to mix with other people or offensive and unacceptable behavior toward others. There hasn't been a more offensive and unacceptable act in American history than the enslavement of African Slaves (as well as the aforementioned genocidal campaign against Native Americans.) This act not only continues to reveal the sociopathic traits of whiteness but it also reinforces the fact that the statement "Lift yourself up by your own bootstraps" is a lie. Without the contributions of African slaves on whose blood, sweat, and tears this country's economy was established, we wouldn't have the world's greatest economy today. Because of chattel slavery where African slaves were bought and sold as property and forced to work for no pay, America was able to export cotton and grow the American economy. Slavery was not the act of slave owners lifting themselves up by their own bootstraps but the sociopathic mental sickness of whiteness, which allowed for the inadequately motivated antisocial behavior of slavery. This exploitation of African slaves led to the establishment of many white millionaires, the building of many institutions, the nursing and the raising of future white slave owners, and the growth of the American economy. The importation of African Slaves stemmed from the need to have a people strong and durable enough to work in the heat for hours. Whites were not capable of doing this themselves. Had whites had to do this work and pay their workers, the American economy would not had been able to grow at such an exponential rate. Thus African Slaves made an incalculable contribution to the establishment of America. Ironically enough, even after this contribution, when African Americans were freed, whites were unwilling to mix with them and that sociopathic trait led to Jim Crow laws and legal segregation. The critic of "lifting one's self by their own bootstraps," is not to belittle the necessity of self determination and resolve. It is vitally important for one to have self-determination to succeed in life. However, for us to suggest that America was founded on individuals who did it all by themselves is fallacy. What is an even bigger fallacy is the belief that America was founded by whites who did it all by themselves. This belief is not just untruthful it is also insincere.

Lifting yourself up by your own bootstraps can further be dispelled by the historical event that was the Great Depression. The Great Depression was the worst economic event in the countries' history. In order for America to survive this economic downturn, President Franklin D Roosevelt constructed the New Deal. This New Deal created programs that would help Americans get back to work, own homes, and lower unemployment (unemployment was also impacted by World War 2.) These government programs and not the pulling up of bootstraps were what helped Americans survive this depression. However, government assistance was not equitably distributed to all Americans. In order for the New Deal to pass, President Roosevelt had to gain the support of Southern politicians who in my opinion had the mental disease of whiteness. These politicians would pass the bill only if this aid did not help African Americans (please read the Color of Law by Richard Rothstein). So not only did whites benefit from government assistance but also this assistance was given to them at a disproportionate rate than other Americans. Ironically enough, the superficial charm and good intelligence of whiteness has created the false narrative that African Americans are lazy and violent. The narrative of the Welfare Queen ran rampant in the 1980s when in actuality whites receive more welfare benefits than African Americans. The narrative of the hyper sexual, hoodie wearing, birth of a nation gangster, and drug dealing super predator has been the narrative given to young black men. However, if we look at history and statistics it tells another story. Michelle Alexander's "The New Jim Crow learned me something (it's a must read.) I learned that White males commit more gang violence, domestic violence, and drunk driving offenses than any other demographic. Not only that, government programs such as affirmative action, which has been advertised to help African Americans and Latinos, has benefited White women the most. The fact that the narrative does not reflect the truth shows the superficial charm and good intelligence that comes with the mental disease of whiteness.

What has furthered my summation that whiteness is a mental disease, which resembles sociopathic traits, is the lack of remorse. As facts about our American history are brought to the forefront we continuously see the lack of remorse and humanity of whites stricken with this mental disease. This act also reinforces my previous statement that the disease of whiteness has nothing to do with being Caucasian because many Caucasian allies (shout out to Killa Mike) have existed throughout our American history. There has been Caucasian Black panthers, activists, and humanitarians who are in the trenches fighting for the soul of this country. They can clearly see the hypocrisy of this country's narrative, the need to renounce their privilege, the need to establish equity for all people as well as the need to reconcile with the sins of the past. To them I say I thank you and love you! (And you invited to the cookout!) However, there are many who neither have remorse of shame when it comes to the inhumane history of America.

Remorse and shame is the least America can have because of its past but there are times where it is hard to find. In a country where we are told to Never Forget 9/11 we are continuously told to get over slavery, Jim Crow, segregation, the assassination of our black heroes, and most importantly get over the idea of reparations. Recently, Mitch McConnell shared that he feels there is no need for reparations because we have shown progress by having our first Black President (a President that was disrespected his 8 years in office and whom Mitch McConnell fought every step of the way.) He also shared that it would be difficult to figure out who legitimately were descendants of slaves (as if last names aren't a good indicator.) Well if we are one of the smartest countries in the world, capable of sending folks into space and being innovators in the tech world, it is hard for me to believe we wouldn't be able to use that brainpower to solve this reparation equation unless of course we weren't really trying to solve it at all.

True remorse and shame would drive folks to make right the horrors of the past regardless of how difficult it may be. True remorse would lead to legislation that specifically helps African Americans and other minorities who were not just exploited at the genesis of this nation but also not given equitable aid when the New Deal and other governmental intervention programs were established. Shame and remorse is not saying that there were good people on both sides when speaking about Charlottesville. Shame and remorse is not rationalizing and normalizing the mental disease of whiteness. It is the commitment to making sure no one in this nation is exploited or feels lesser than. However, throughout history there has been a lack of remorse and shame. The disease of whiteness has led to whites being unreliable.

Martin Luther King is one of the greatest revolutionaries to ever grace this earth. His movement of non-violence and civil rights along with his vision of the beloved community was the catalyst for many of the positive changes we have in the country. It was his belief that through non-violence the white man would be able to see the error of his ways and change. I believe this belief is noble and admirable. But I believe Martin Luther King may have miscalculated the strength of white morality and failed to diagnose the mental disease of whiteness. There is not historical basis to which this belief can be connected. There is no time in our American History where white morale (as a whole) was the foundation that helped marginalized persons of color progress without there being a benefit to whites. History clearly shows that whites have a track record of exploitation, violence, genocide, and lies. When I began to reflect on American history and the actions of whites, I have found a track record of inadequately motivated antisocial behavior, superficial charm and good intelligence, unreliability, untruthfulness and insincerity, lack of remorse and shame, poor judgment and failure to learn by experience. Thus I believe that whiteness is a mental disease.

The reason why I feel that it is important to identify whiteness as a mental disease lies in how we move forward. For far too long we have been complacent with the movement of justice and humanity because we have felt that white morale was a mandatory component to this movement. While I admit that the restoration and progression of this country requires an all hand on deck approach, I don't believe we should allow this progress to be held hostage by something we by and large have not seen. I further believe that if we viewed whiteness as a mental disease we would understand how silly that proposition is. If we diagnosed whiteness as a mental disease we wouldn't wait for white folk to gain sense, we would take the onus on ourselves to repair this country and move forward while simultaneously offering help to those who are stricken with this disease. To make the self-healing of a mentally ill person a prerequisite for the restoration and progress of a nation is at the very least irresponsible and at most foolhardy. Those who are mentally ill need help and not power. I believe we must be patient with the expectations that those who suffer from the disease of whiteness (which isn't a disease that only Caucasians have, many African Americans and other minorities have this sickness also) will get better but for all of us in the majority who don't have this sickness, we most move forward with hast to fix and improve this country. Those of us who realize that there is no need for hierarchy in the human race and as humans we have a responsibility to make whole all those who have unjustly suffered in the formation of this country, need not seek permission from the mental ill to do so. Big momma said it like this; "WHEN YOU KNOW BETTER YOU DO BETTER!" Let's not wait for someone else to do better because there are too many lives at stake. So to all the Caucasians not stricken with this disease and to every minority not stricken, lets not wait for the sick to come to their senses to move forward. Let us band together and do what is right and then help those who have this disease get better. If we wait for them, we will never get there.

6
Gang, Gang, Gang !

Where I grew up in Bed-Stuy, there was nothing but Bloods. The dudes that I was weary of because I was told they cut people happened to be really cool (and they cut certain people lol). Many of them either lived in my building or a block away and we all hung out in front of my building. Each one of them had mothers and siblings and cared about things. We went to parties together where many of them were great dancers. We also played sports together especially handball, which was how my friends and I became really close to all the Bloods in my neighborhood. There is no denying that crimes were committed, there was jail time and people got jumped from time to time, but by in large these were teenage boys and girls who were trying to figure out who they were in a world that rejected them. They had parents who loved and cared about them, many were intelligent, and all were looking for unity and love.

Across the street at Boys and Girls High School, there were quite a few gangs since students came from different neighborhoods. Whether in LA (which is the birth place of the Pirus, Brims, Bloods and Crips) Chicago (birth place of the Vice Lords, P.Stone Rangers, Latin Kings and many other gangs) or New York, being in a gang largely stems from where you live. Your connection to your neighborhood dictated what gang you would be in unless you were initiated in jail or had family ties. Even if you weren't officially in a gang (like myself) simply being from a neighborhood or hanging with gang members made you guilty by association.

Our Principal Frank Mickens wasn't having foolishness of any kind at Boys and Girls so any fighting in or around school would get you a 15-day suspension and your schedule cut in half (that would mean that you left school early but there was no way for you to graduate on time.) Depending on what the circumstances were behind the fight, you could even get kicked out of the school so fighting at Boys and Girls was rare. More often than not you were in a class with students who were affiliated with multiple gangs and you had to do class assignments and group projects together. This allowed students to understand that despite being from a different gang or neighborhood, most students weren't different from one another. My lunchroom table was like the United Nation of gangs. There were Bloods, Crips and Latin Kings all eating together, joking on each other, arguing about sports, playing Uno and of course playing spades! No matter what happened outside of school, there was a mutual respect of humanity amongst all the people at our table and certain groups in the school.

This is not to romanticize what gang life and gang culture has become! Though the origins of the Bloods and Crips are noble (Community Resistance In Progress and Brotherly Love Overcomes Oppression and Destruction), these organizations have evolved to a self-destructive force in our community. Lil Monster said it best when he said, "Gang banging is a death style not a lifestyle." Many of our greatest thinkers, warriors and future politicians have died or have been locked up way before their purpose could be actualized due to being in gangs. There is a need and subsequently has been a movement to reform the purpose and meaning of gang life especially in the black community. Many former gang members are going back into the community to help save the lives of teens entrenched in gang violence.

But this chapter thus far suffers from what America has made gang culture. Gang culture in America is NOT a black problem it is an American problem. Though the Bloods and Crips are the face of gang violence in America, white gangs have been a huge part of American culture since its inception. Gangs such as the Aryan nation and the Hell's Angels have been organizing and terrorizing the U.S. for years (don't make me get started with the KKK.) And this is not an indictment on any gang, this is to acknowledge the fact if we are going to call out Bloods and Crips for their negative impact on society we need to call out all gangs especially because black gangs aren't the most violent. When reading Michelle Alexander's "The New Jim Crow," I was blown away when I learned white men commit more gang violence than any other race in America. This death style that Lil Monsta spoke of is not just a black issue, in fact it is actually a bigger issue for whites in this country.

What makes gang culture dangerous isn't just the violence; it's also the mindset. The mindset that what you and your crew are riding for is more important than the community can destroy your crew and the community. And though this mindset makes sense for organizations like the Bloods and Crips due to their members by and large feeling rejected by their communities it has absolutely no place in other arenas. The arena where the gang mindset has been the most consequential in American society recently has been in the arena of politics. In Kendrick Lamar's song *Hood Politics*, be brilliantly pens the words "Ain't nothing new but a flow of new DemoCrips and ReBloodicans/ Red State versus Blue State who are you governing." This gang mindset has seeped into our politics in a way that has cost more lives than any gang war ever could. Whether Democrat or Republican, the partisan divide has become so stark that Congress has been useless in helping the country progress. Irresponsible comments such as" Democrats want to take away your guns and hamburgers" along with "all Republicans are racists," have filled the airwaves. Bills and policies have been voted on party lines not because there is a fundamental belief that it will help the country but simply because the DemoCrips are down for their gang and the ReBloodicans are down for theirs.

We have seen the consequence of this gang mindset with the shutting down of the country. It didn't matter that the constituents of the politicians were hurting and couldn't pay their rent or mortgage. It didn't matter that those who relied on the government for their fundamental needs couldn't get it. What mattered was the gang. There has been more bipartisanship seen between street gangs in rap music than there has been in congress in recent years. The gang mindset is most pronounced in the Republican Party. The OG Mitch McConnell not only stone walled the submission of a Supreme Court Justice but he also hasn't brought forth common sense gun reform to the Senate for a vote simply because its coming from the other side. As I previously stated, we average a mass shooting a day, which has not been discriminating. Whether it is black folk at church, young white kids in schools, our LGBTQIA+ brothers and sisters at a party, Latinos at stores, or people at music festivals, gun violence has impacted every fabric of America. However the response from Republican representatives have been "I believe in the second amendment." It is vitally important for us to separate Republican representatives from their constituents because many people who vote republican are good folk. They simply believe the government shouldn't be all in your business and take all your bread. I can respect the philosophical differences of each party. However, Republican politicians try to scare their constituents by saying they are after your guns and your hamburgers. As if we can't both have common sense gun reform (say like Australia who has only had a mass shooting once) and still maintain an individuals right to bare arms. Not to mention the fact that the AR 15 was not created when the second amendment was written so having a musket or a six-shooter to protect yourself is vastly different than having a wartime assault rifle at the ready. But no matter how many lives are lost the ReBloodicans are still standing firm. This is due to the fact that the NRA funds many of the ReBloodicans. So, they would rather get paid and our people die than stand up for the lives of the constituents who elected them.

    Another gang mindset found in our politics is being a rider even when your peoples are wrong. Like if me and my mans are out and he starts a fight, I'm going to fight along side him and then when we get home we will fight. In the ReBloodicans party we have seen the most dangerous president in our history say and do some of the most outrageous things in the history of this country and ReBloodicans have either defended him or remained quiet. Whether it's using government money to line his own pockets, disrespecting 5 star generals, spewing racist, transphobic, islamophobic rhetoric, publicly disrespecting women, lying on national television, doctoring weather reporters, or siding with Russia over our own intelligence, ReBloodican politicians have not done enough to stand up for their constituents or for the values of this country. They care more about riding for their congressional crew and president than this country or their constituents.

DemoCrips have also had their flaws. Though they claim to have the higher moral ground, there hasn't been enough action to prove this. Just recently Newark, New Jersey has had a water purification crisis with both a democratic Mayor and Governor. This is after the national crisis that occurred in Ferguson. My critic of the DemoCrips is not what they say or even how they vote but what they do. The in fighting and confusion of the overall direction of the party (do they want to be liberal or moderate) can be likened to the infighting between LA Crips in the 90s. Watching the first Democratic debate was strange in that it seemed Barack Obama's presidency was on trial as opposed to candidates stating their platforms. When we look at the Democratic cities in the country there is still issues with racism, sexism, islamophobia and the like. This is not to say there hasn't been progress, but it is to say there hasn't been enough. There is also a lot of money that is saturated in the Democratic Party that doesn't always allow them to completely represent the values of their constituents. Whether it's blue or red we have a serious gang problem with our political system.

Killa Mike shared that African Americans in this country had their greatest form of prosperity 7 years after the civil war as Republicans. Subsequently we have become Democrats and haven't had the same prosperity since. In my neighborhood there was no fundamental reason for hating Crips except for the fact that they were Crips. We were told that we were supposed to hate them so we did. It became real when we started fighting them and people on both sides got hurt. The ignorant rhetoric of both parties creates an us vs them dynamic that has split this country into Red and Blue. Political conversations cannot take place without their being an attack on someone's character. All the while our political representatives aren't even fighting for the causes we sent them to Washington for. The money in this political system allows them to rep the gang in a completely different way.

Ultimately, when the Republicans repeal Obama care without a replacement, they won't be affected because they don't even use the same healthcare system as their constituents. They will simply be taking away healthcare from the very people who put them in office. The gang is more important than the community. The Democrats may have a moral high ground but when in office they still have left much to be desired. They have so many people tryna be OG right now that they set tripping. Whether it is in politics or in our communities, what we, as Americans must remember is that gangs never outnumber the people. If we want this gang mentality out of our politics we need to elect politicians who are more about the community then they are about the gang. I love my Blood homies and Crips homies. I understand their plight and their reason to band together in a world that rejects them. For politicians to act gang like, knowing that their decisions literally can mean the lives and livelihood of our people, means they're the worse gang in our nation. Their decisions have cost more lives than any gang ever could and what is worse, they ain't about that life. As constituents we need to hold them accountable for whom they are supposed to be and keep the fake gangstas out of our politics.

7

We Rep Different

The Completely Sporadic Thoughts of a Black Brooklyn Intellect

One of my ex girlfriends used to go to church 6 days a week. I couldn't understand why a teenage girl would spend 6 days of her week at church until I went. Monday was Mime, Tuesday Teen Counsel, Wednesday they were off, Thursday was youth choir, Friday was Teen Canteen and on the weekends there was church service. I quickly realized that in order to see my girlfriend I would have to go to church (MESSAGE) and that decision would eventually change my life.

The first time I went to Emmanuel Baptist Church was on a Thursday evening during youth choir. The teens were practicing songs they would be ministering that weekend and they sounded horrible. Not because they couldn't sing, they had amazing voices, but because they were woefully unprepared. Going into the weekend I was extremely nervous because I knew that if they sang on Sunday morning the same way they sang on Thursday night, the results would be ugly. On Sunday the teens showed up and showed out. They did an amazing job and had the freedom to worship God in their own way. They sang, rapped (shout out to the Youth Thugs) mimed, and acted. It wasn't hard for me to now realize why my ex went to church everyday. It eventually became something I did myself long after we broke up.

The Lay Pastor of the Youth at that time was Jocelyn Mann, a loving, strong woman who has been my mentor since I walked through the church doors. She could also throw down (cook) so on days I didn't have money to eat she would either cook or buy food. For a young man entering his 20s it was hard to share with anyone when I was in need, but she provided for me and allowed me to keep my dignity. She was also a phenomenal creative, penning all the skits, created most of the mimes and wrote some of the best sermons I have never heard. I joined Emmanuel Baptist Church because Jocelyn Mann loved me and fed me for no reason!

The youth ministry introduced me to church and allowed me to feel like I had a place. From there I was introduced to the Frontliners men ministry where I met some amazing father figures in the form of Jonathan Hicks, Tony Canady, Bryant Smith and of course my Senior Pastor Rev Anthony L. Trufant (there are tons more but let's keep it at 4.) Reverend Trufant is a true revolutionary who not only grew with his parishioners to mega church status in his time there, but also moved the church forward in its theology and activism. I knew that Emmanuel Baptist Church was my church when Reverend Trufant said during the invitation (when visitors are invited join the church) that we believed there were multiple ways people could get into heaven and he believed that Christianity in his opinion was the best way, but not the only way.

I was like WHHHHAAATTTTTT?????!!!?????

I never heard a pastor say that let alone during an invitation. Most pastors I've heard would say there was only one true religion. That statement from Reverend Trufant made me appreciate him for his boldness and made me want to learn more.

Obviously there was something he knew that none of these other pastors were telling us.

It was Jocelyn's mentorship that got me to come to church and Rev's revolutionary boldness that intrigued me, but it was Reverend Shareka Newton's preaching that made me feel like I could actually be a preacher myself. On one particular Sunday she preached a sermon that basically said that there are times God will allow things to be taken from us to make room for us to get newer and better things. The intro to her sermon centered on how much she loved Jay-Z and how she felt when her Reasonable Doubt tape popped. The sermon was masterful and it left me with an equation in my head. I thought to myself she loves Jay-Z and Jesus and she was able to preach about it. I too love Jay-Z and Jesus… maybe I can do the same thing.

I'd read the bible for myself and realized that there were TONS of stories in the bible that are different from what I was told. Essentially the bible is a love story about a God who helped an oppressed people get free. There were countless times that those free people wanted to revert back to slavery in one way or another but God continued to love them. There was a lot of breaking up and getting back together. But all in all it's a love story about freedom.

While I was considering my call I joined 20/30s, which is a small group for people between the ages of 20 and 39. I became a member of Goodness (Damali, Aaron, Torie, Desmond, Ike, Khori ya already know) and went on trips all over the country to help survivors of Hurricane Ike and Katrina. Going to Emmanuel Baptist Church, took me from a young man who was guarded and developed me into a man who could freely love and be loved. That is a miracle I will always be grateful for.

When I decided to answer the call to ministry of course I went to Jocelyn first. She advised me to set up a meeting with Reverend Trufant, which I did. Without getting into too much detail, this meeting led me on a path which included reading a book, outlining the bible, writing a spiritual autobiography, meeting with the deacons and preaching a trial sermon. Once I did all of that, I was officially a minister and had 6 months to a year to go to Seminary. I would end up going to Princeton Theological Seminary and upon graduating I then had to have an ordination exam in order for me to become a licensed Reverend. My big homies Reverend Pamela Saxton and Mike Saxton were instrumental in me getting through this process and keeping me sane. Pam is my spiritual big sister who is like my guardian angel. She is my backbone. When working at the church Renee Jarvis and Terri Canady (Tony's sister) adopted me along with Charlotte and Cory so to say I have been loved and encouraged by my church is an understatement. So when I represent being a Christian it stems from the love of my church, my reading and toiling with the word of God, my learning, arguing and evolution through seminary and my knowledge of the living God found in the world today. So when I rep being Christian it may look different than how others rep it.

- I come from a church that teaches our congregants to read the bible for themselves.
- I believe that Christianity isn't they only religion that will make it to heaven especially considering the fact that Jesus was a Jew and Ishmael's lineage is also blessed (our Islamic brothers and sisters.) My favorite revolutionaries also happen to be Malcolm X and Muhammad Ali, so when I go on to glory I look forward to rapping with them.
- I was taught from Seminary that Israel was occupied by Rome who persecuted the Israelites. Not until the Edict of Milan in 313 did Rome stop the killing and persecution of Christians so the fact that the Roman Catholic Church is the official authority on a religion they persecuted is strange to me.
- I learned that the image of Jesus that was hanging in my crib was not true or historically accurate (look up Cesare Borgia). Jesus was a brown skinned Afro-Asian man who would have had trouble getting on a plane

after 9/11 and definitely would had gotten caught up in this Muslim ban.

- Jesus was a Jewish reformer who opposed the Roman rule. He was a revolutionary who understood the power of women, ran with a crew who later ran on him, suffered and died.
- Christianity has never been a white religion but was repackaged as such. This faith was built on the persecution and liberation of black and brown bodies and then popularized by the very institution that persecuted them. It was later weaponized to subjugate the very people who originated the faith in the first place making many mistake it for a Roman religion.

So, when I say I'm a Christian, this is the context, mindset, love and energy I'm coming with. It's a love for liberation, a love for all people (shout out to my LGBTQIA+ folk and races of all nations) and a desire to share the love of God I found in my church.

NOW! How I rep and how others have repped Christianity is very different. One of the most problematic aspects of the Christian faith is the fact that though 83% of Americans identify as Christian there is no true definition to what that means. Someone can go to church on Sunday, walk down an aisle and profess to be Christian. Christianity has become so vague that depending on the individual; you may not know what Christianity stands for. Some Christians believe in baptism by immersion and others don't. Some believe you have to be 12 or older to get baptized and others get baptized as babies. There are progressive Christians and conservative Christians. There are Christians who have been saved for 50 years and others who were saved last night. Christianity has become one of the illusive terms in the English lexicon. So when I rep being a Christian and others rep it, there are times where we are repping different.

For example, what exactly is an Evangelical? I hear about them all the time in politics but I'm not sure that I've ever met one. Based on how the media portrays them and how they seemingly voted in this recent election I'm far from an Evangelical! But since Evangelicals fall under the Christian banner many people believe that all Christians believe as Evangelicals do but that couldn't be farther from the truth.

Many politicians claim to be Christian because its marketable yet there is nothing Christian about their policies. When Donald Trump quoted 2nd Corinthians 3:17 at a conservative college, it was obvious he hadn't read the scripture let alone the bible. Ironically the scripture he read states, "Now the Lord is the Spirit, and where the Spirit of the Lord is, there is freedom." The bible also states in Deuteronomy 10:18, "He (God) ensures that orphans and widows receive justice. He shows love to the foreigners living among you and gives them food and clothing." However, there are many Christian politicians who have turned a blind eye to the suffering of migrates on a southern border. In Leviticus 19:34 and Deuteronomy 10:19, we are commanded to treat the foreigner living among us as a native born and to love the foreigner since we ourselves were foreigners at one point but that doesn't seem to be in the politics of some so called "Christian," politicians. The love and compassion that is abundantly and plentifully found in the bible is hard to find in the law and order rhetoric recited by many "Christian," politicians. There was no love or compassion in the mandatory minimum laws created in the 90s. There was no love and compassion found in the Jim Crow laws of the 60s. There was no love and compassion during World War 2 when Japanese Americans were forced to live in concentration camps. And there definitely wasn't love and compassion in the act of slavery or manifest destiny. In fact, slave owners only wanted certain parts of the bible read so slaves would not know its liberating power. Now we have false claiming Christian politicians who neither know the word of God or the God of the word. These false claimers shame God with their spinelessness and their cowardice. These false claimers pervert the word of God for their own purposes and care not about the people of God. These false claimers sit in church on Sundays and open their bibles only for the photo op but when its time for them to vote on legislation that will help the least of these, they don't.

I completely understand why Christianity turns some people off because there are too many false claimers to know who the real ones are. When I say I'm a Christian people think I'm a narrow minded pro life, patriarchal, bible thumping, non-welcoming and affirming hypocritical man who doesn't listen to reason. This is what the revolutionary loving movement of Jesus has been reduced to. When I engage with people I share the love of my church and the love of Jesus Christ that I have experienced first hand. I also share my experiences understanding their skepticism because everyone repping Christianity ain't always about this Christian life. But Jesus knew this so he gave everyone this little scripture, Matthew 7:15-20:

> *"Beware of false Prophets, who come to you in sheep's clothing, but inwardly they are ravenous wolves. You will know them by their fruits. Do men gather grapes from thornbushes or figs from thistles? Even so, every good tree bears good fruit, but a bad tree bears bad fruit… Therefore by their fruits you know them."*

The Completely Sporadic Thoughts of a Black Brooklyn Intellect

Everybody wanna claim Christian but do your actions match up to it. When I think about my church and the lives changed, the love shared, and the improvement in our community I know we repping right. The bible says they will know we are Christians by our love and my church has always loved me. But the way these politicians live their lives and vote, I know we don't rep the same thing. They may claim to be Christian, but WE REP DIFFERENT.

8

FUCK YOUR

STARES!!!!

What you looking at me for? I didn't come to stay!

(Maya Angelou thank you and I love you!)

One of the most important and vital questions you can ask someone growing up in the hood also happens to be the first line of track number 10 on Reasonable Doubt; That question…

FRIEND OR FOE YOU STATE YOUR BIZ?

This question is vital because if you are unable to decipher your friends from your foes you will not survive in the hood. Because of this, one must constantly be aware of one's surroundings. We are told that 85% of communication is non-verbal so if someone's handshake isn't matching their smile (Beanie Sigel – *Feel it in the air*) there is reason to be alarmed. There are tons of signs that can make you question someone's friend or foe status. In my opinion, the first indicator is the stare.

Staring is very intimate and intrusive. In the hood, you try not to stare at people you don't know because that action can immediately be mistaken for a challenge. After about 2 seconds of looking at someone, you must make your intentions known or look away. Otherwise, you will get some version of Friend or foe. More than likely someone is gonna ask you, "What the fuck are you looking at?" Being stared at by someone you don't know in an environment where self-preservation is key, is never a comfortable feeling. When someone used to look at me I thought they either wanted to challenge me, was plotting on me or worst yet, was judging me. The older I got, the more the latter was the case. Stares I received stemmed more from judgment than from anything else. As I left Bed-Stuy and ventured out into different cities, towns and countries, I quickly realized that no matter what I did or what I was wearing those stares never went away. This was alarming and unsettling for me because when I was younger I was told not to judge a book by its cover. My momma told me what someone has on doesn't matter, what matters is who that person is inside. Momma then told me not to wear hoodies, and not to walk with my friends in the group because of how it looked. And this is not an indictment on my mother because she was simply trying to protect me in a world structured around the subjugation of black and brown bodies; however, judgment based on aesthetics is socially normative. People judge you on how you look. The theory is, the more you adopt a Western European aesthetic, (the whiter you are, the more you wear suits, the straighter your hair is and the lighter you are) the more American society accepts you. The problem is some of us can't afford suits, our hair is naturally curly and many of us come in lusciously dark and beautifully Nubian colors (get into it!) Moreover, some of us don't want to conform to those aesthetics because they don't represent our true selves.

What is frightening though is how many people compromise who they are to fit this socially normative western European aesthetic in the pursuit of acceptance just to be rejected and judged anyway. You trade in your hoodie for a suit just to be stared at and ridiculed for looking out of place. You burn your scalp and avoid the rain, all in an effort to keep your hair in an altered state. You bleach your skin and try desperately to not speak with your native accent or vernacular in order to be accepted, all for you to be judged and looked over. Until finally it hits you and you realize that no matter how much you try to confirm to this socially normative western European aesthetic, some people will still never accept you or be comfortable around you. No matter how much you try, you can't escape the stares!

    I say this because I currently hold a Bachelors degree and two Masters degrees but while I pursued them I still got stares. (I still get stares now!) Whether I wore a suit or a hoodie the uneasiness and judgment from others was still very much apparent in those places. I'm from the hood where I had to read stares for my livelihood so walking through the hallways of Princeton Theological Seminary and feeling those stares was quite interesting. This place where everyone was supposed to be working through their calling from God, was still full of the judgmental stares that I got in the hood. I was told those judgmental stares come from a lack of accomplishment but I had a bachelors degree and a ministers license. I was told those stares came from what I wore but there were times I had on suits or robes and still got them. I was told that those stares came from a lack of intelligence and yet I found that many of my white colleagues were far less academically astute (they were dumb yall) than my minority peers.

Very early on in my life I had to come to a few realizations. My first realization was that most likely I would be dead or in jail simply because I was a black man. Another realization was that if I did manage to survive and avoid jail, people who wanted to villianize me would always question my character and personhood, so fuck them and their thoughts. Lastly, I realized that no matter how hard I tried to be accepted into this Western European aesthetically driven society they will only see me as the chorus of the song from "The Story of OJ" by Jay-Z. So I reconciled very early on to be my motherfucking self no matter how uncomfortable it made other people. So I wore hoodies and

Jordans whenever I felt like it (its hood now – Lupe Fiasco.) I spoke and speak in any vernacular I see fit and make sure that my authentic self is expressed in the best possible way and if people want to judge with their stares, FUCK THEM AND FUCK THEIR STARES!!

    Identifying and naming this Western European aesthetically driven society is important because we are taught that this is the best aesthetic to emulate in order to achieve success. Therefore, people sacrifice and abandon parts of who they are in order to fit this aesthetic. Some parents raise their kids to fit this aesthetic in hopes that they will be successful even if it requires the assassination of part of that child's authentic identity. When we follow this blueprint and are still stared at, judged and unsuccessful at being accepted by society we feel horrible. Not only are we rejected though we did what society told us to do but also we are rejected in a form that's not even our true selves. We scarified that to be accepted. So, when we see someone else who hasn't been trapped into fitting this aesthetic we immediately give him or her the same stares we hated. But we do it not only in judgment but also in envy. Wishing we could be that authentic but we allowed society to take it from us but this person has the audacity to be themselves despite what society told them to be.

    Being in a Western European aesthetically driven society is just one way we are expected to conform. We are also in a hetero-normative, patriarchal, gender role assigning society as well. Which means if you aren't heterosexual, male, and if you don't act in accordance with the roles society gives your gender that was assigned to you at birth you will be judged and get those stares. The LGBTQIA+ community is not a community I can say I truly understand. I am not informed enough about their plight to speak outside of my own convictions. However, what I can say is our brothers and sisters in the LGBTQIA+ community deserve to be seen and loved without stares and judgments. I remember feeling that the task of understanding what cisgender meant and figuring out what all those letters mean was daunting. But that was spoken out of my privilege and my ignorance. If we all had to label the uniqueness of our identity and sexuality in order that we could be understood there wouldn't be enough letters for all of us. Maybe that is why many of us who consider ourselves heterosexual are misunderstood. There were times where I stared in curiosity, in envy and in judgment and for that I apologize and say FUCK MY STARES! I also say I love you! I may not understand everything but I am an ally and I am willing and ready to learn. Please be gentle with my ignorance.

Ultimately, stares are a threat to our existence no matter where you come from. Unless that stare is followed by an "I'm sorry I thought you were someone I knew," "Excuse me can I ask you a question?" or something positive we need to self examine why we are staring at someone. Whether its teenage kids kissing on the train, a young man in a hoodie, a trans-woman in heels, or a girl burping after drinking soda we can keep our judgments and stares to ourselves. We need to address the issues stemming from this Western European aesthetically driven society as well as the issues brought about through this hetero-normative, patriarchal, transphobic, gender role assigning society as well. These things create chains that keep us from being our authentic selves. When we can't be our authentic selves it is impossible to love ourselves. When it is impossible to love ourselves it is impossible to love others who don't look like us. When you can't be who you really want to be because of society, you subconsciously soothe that pain by convincing yourself that no one else can be themselves either because of that same restriction. When you begin to see others fight back and are actually celebrated for being their authentic selves, it's hard to celebrate them knowing you weren't able to do that yourself. But we must! Why?? Because within their fight lies the true blueprint that we need to follow; the blueprint of self-actuality. You are not going to be able to be you without a fight so when you see someone else being himself or herself celebrate them. Applaud the person who is bold enough to love who they choose regardless of what society says. Applaud the person who will make sure you address them in the matter that makes them feel comfortable. Applaud the person that will wear whatever the fuck he wants whether you think he is a thug or not. And while you are doing that, work on being and loving your true authentic unique self. Lets break free of the restrictions this society has given us and be ourselves. Walk proudly in your own skin and existence regardless of how others may feel. And if they stare... well... FUCK THEM AND FUCK THEIR STARES!!

The Completely Sporadic Thoughts of a Black Brooklyn Intellect

9
Sorry we fucked up!

Why does society take so much issue with teenagers? It's almost like becoming a teen makes you liable for all the ills of the world. I remember being confused by how I was being treated and how the "world," worked. None of it made sense to me. All of a sudden I was the reason why society was going to hell in a hand basket and my very valid questions about why we had to do certain things were viewed as signs of laziness. Apparently I had no idea how good I had it, the music I listened to was trash and my generation was nowhere near as good as it's predecessor. I guess they didn't understand how hard it was to be a teenager. I was told that they too had been teenagers at some point in their lives but maybe they had forgotten what it was like to be a teen. Maybe they forgot about having to figure out who you are and want to be in the mist of peer pressure and parental harassment. Maybe they forgot about puberty, having your heartbroken for the first time but still having to go to class. Maybe they forgot about wanting to have more freedom but still having to take care of siblings and work jobs to take care of bills that weren't theirs. Maybe they forgot how it feels to be picked on and jumped going to and coming from school. Maybe they forgot about taking classes and tests that have no real purpose in your life. Or maybe they just don't care.

As a 34-year-old man I truly can say I don't understand much of the new music that comes out nowadays but I don't bash it because I remember hearing adults bash the hip-hop and R&B music that has been the soundtrack of my life. As I began to teach I wanted to make sure I remembered what it was like to be a teenage student. I remembered that kid who cried when he turned 18 because up to that point, that was the biggest miracle he ever experienced. I wanted to connect with any and every student who felt the same way I felt when I was a teen. That's why I chose for my first year of teaching to be in a high school.

In New York City, in order for you to graduate from High School you have to pass exams called the Regents. There is a Regents exam for every major subject and for others as well. As a high school student I hated homework but I was a great test taker so I easily passed my Regents. When you are a high school teacher, much of your success is correlated with the results of the Regents exams. You can be a horrible teacher but if you can teach students how to pass the Regents, you will have a job. One day, a student of mine needed help studying for her Algebra Regents exam. Though I taught Global History and English, I helped her study for the exam. In the middle of working on one of the questions, my student looked up at me and said, "Mr, when am I gonna use any of this in real life? Why do I have to learn this?" And I looked at her and said, "I have no idea." Honestly, after passing the math regent, I had no functional purpose for most of the math I learned in high school. I also felt that simply saying, "Its gonna help you in the future!" was not factual enough to say if she wasn't going to major in math in college. The question she asked that day was a relevant question that really needs to be researched. Why do we force our children to learn arbitrary things that they won't use in life and be upset with them when they ask us why they have to learn it? Many of us asked the same questions when we were their age. As I took a deeper look into how far off the mark our educational system is from lessons you need to learn in actual life, I realized that its not the kids who are fucking up, its us the adults. So, to all the teens that are reading this book (sorry for the profanity and) Sorry we fucked up!

As adults we have fucked up in many ways and our kids deserve an apology from us. Not simply for the horrible education system but for most of the things going on in this world. What makes it worse is the fact that we look at them and make it seem like their questioning and rejection of some of the nonsensical things we call normative makes them the problem. As if we ourselves didn't struggle with these same issues when we were their age but eventually conformed. But since we are already talking about education, lets take a deeper dive into the mess that is our education system.

In New York City, students spend around 7 hours a day in school with the goal of learning. But, what exactly are they learning and how is their intelligence being measured? Teens are coming to school with PhDs in street awareness, college degrees in figurative language and are fluent in body language. Yet if they can't remember that Y=MX+B they can be regarded as stupid. Additionally, students are coming to schools with real world issues. Some have not eaten, others are worried about evictions and some are dealing with real loss and yet if they can't remember the difference between SIN, COS, and TAN they are viewed as incompetent. Where are the foundational classes such as cooking, trades, farming, taxes, credit and the like? I know that many schools have included such classes in their curriculum and they are to be applauded. But more schools need to follow suit. Imagine if our school system taught in a manner that reflected Maslow's hierarchy of needs where not only are their current needs being met but we are creating environments where their future needs are as well. There is no reason why students can't get a barber license and cosmetology certifications while in high school so they are marketable right out of high school. There is also no reason why the purpose of learning something shouldn't be readily apparent to an inquisitive teen. We shouldn't rob our teens of their why simply in an effort to have them conform to the broken inefficient systems we no longer question. Your children deserve more and we need to do more. It is our responsibility to make sure our teens are encouraged to be change agents. It is also our responsibility to give them the space to be those agents. If we aren't doing that we are fucking up and we are messing up the children. In the great words of Lupe Fiasco:

"DON'T MESS UP THE CHILDREN"

Education is not the only area where we fucking up. When we blame teens for being the bane of society when we have this type of society, we are deceiving ourselves. Our children inherit the world they live in! So if this society is messed up it is either due to the adults living in it making bad decisions or adults conforming to it. Granted there are a lot of things the youth take for granted. They squander many opportunities most adults wish they had. But adults have also squandered opportunities, made youthful mistakes, took things for granted and had to learn things the hard way as well. You know what our teens didn't bring us.... DONALD TRUMP! Our youth didn't bring us trillions of dollars into credit card debt, college debt or homeownership debt. Our teens are not the reason why rent is too damn high. They aren't the reason why we have global warming. Our teens didn't create nor do they regulate the broken judicial system they find themselves entangled in. Our teens can't vote so the political mess this country is in is laid squarely on our shoulders. When we look at what our society is today instead of blaming the youth we should apologize and say sorry we fucked up!

Our kids don't deserve Trump, nor do they deserve having social security coming out of their little check when they will never see that money again. Our teens shouldn't be pressured in to trying to figure out what they want to be for the rest of their lives at the age of 18 because not many of us knew at that age. We put pressure on them because college is expensive but instead of putting pressure on teens we should be putting pressure on the colleges! There is no reason why college should be as high as it is.

Students who go to college should also be able to file for bankruptcy if they default on loans the same way grown adults can. The fact that it is normative for students to take out student loans and put themselves into thousands of dollars in debt all for the sake of pursuing the American dream, shows how much we fucked up. Our teens don't deserve our blame they deserve our apology.

Social media has been a major cause of criticism for our youth. They seemingly put anything on social media. They yearn for attention and acceptance from a platform that is not truly real. All those likes under that picture doesn't mean people actually like you and all those friends you have on Facebook aren't your real ones. However, most of us adults have the same issues. If we were honest with ourselves we would willingly admit that had we had social media in our youth we would probably be worse. So, maybe our teens need a little more compassion and a little less judgment. Many of us yearn for the love and attention of folk who don't care about us. Some of us are looking for self-validation through others.

Instead of condemning our youth maybe we should talk and share our stories more. We would realize that we are not as different was the decades mislead us to believe. Additionally it's hard to have disdain for someone you interact with. These conversations are important because many teens feel adults don't like them. They can feel the disdain and some feel hate. So what happens when you begin to hate and resent the very people you are supposed to protect and educate? In the great words of Lupe Fiasco:

"DON'T MESS UP THE CHILDREN"

2 months after I graduated from undergrad I got my minister's license. My senior pastor then told me that I had 6 months to a year to go to seminary. I told my mother that after I graduated with my undergrad degree I would get a job and help her out. The plan was to just go to a local seminary and work. I knew that I wouldn't have been able to get my degree if it wasn't for my mom so I was down to help her. Then I went to meet with my executive

pastor. When she asked me what seminary I was thinking about going to I simply said Union because it's close. I also told her I wanted to help take care of my mother and she then said words that forever changed my life. She said, "It's not your job to take care of your mother!" At first I was immediately offended! What does she mean it's not my job! Of course it is! My mother gave me life! Reading my face she clarified. She said, "It's not your job to sacrifice your future to take care of your mother now. It is different if she was sick or couldn't take care of herself but she can. Your job is to build yourself up so that when she can no longer take care of herself you will have the foundation to take care of her. If you sacrifice your future now, you won't be able to help her when she really needs you. Focus on yourself now so you can help her when she needs you!"

Those words broke the mental generational chains that constricted me. It was not my responsibility to sacrifice my potential to pay off the debt of someone else. As a matter of fact, in order for me to truly make the impact in the lives of my loved ones

I had to focus on my success. Only after that could I reach back and help my family. Also that should be the goal for every parent. Not to bring their children up in poverty and have them help out when they are old enough but for them to build themselves up to the best of their ability. One of the most harmful ways we are fucking up the lives of our teens is passing down the obligation of our debt to them. Teens are asked to sacrifice their dreams and future to help their parents make their ends meet. This is not placing blame on parents and adults. My mom is my heroine and sacrificed a lot for me to get to where I am. There are a multitude of unfortunate events that could lead to parents leaning on their children for financial support. But we have to acknowledge that debt should not be the inheritance that we give our children. If we are doing that we are fucking up! If you ask kids in poverty what is the first thing they will do when they get money, their answer is always getting their mother a house. Embedded in children is the desire to help out their family and community. Likewise, I don't believe that parents have kids with the idea that the children will alleviate their debt but it has been part of the generational curse of poverty.

In the past farmers both black and white would have children and require them to work the land. When schools became an option for children many were only allowed to go to school if it didn't interfere with their farm work. During harvest season, school was not an option. This limited their education and limited their opportunities of leaving those farms. Now instead of farms we have debt. Before a teen can fully spread their wings and actualize their dreams the reality of debt and bad credit shoots their hopes down seemingly before they can get off the ground. As adults we need to allow our teens to be themselves and soar. Let's not require them to fix the financial mistakes we have made. Let us allow them to soar and encourage them along the way. Only after they become their best selves can they come back and make the impact they are truly meant to make in our society. Our children need to question our society because our society is messed up. They need to be encouraged to change it because it needs to be changed. At this rate, we will have nothing to give our kids but a debt filled, climate changing, self-destructive country with an idiot as a president all the while blaming them for the mess we are giving them.

In the great words of Lupe Fiasco:

"DON'T MESS UP THE CHILDREN"

We have some important conversations we need to have with our youth and I believe the first words we should tell them is, "Sorry We Fucked UP!"

The Completely Sporadic Thoughts of a Black Brooklyn Intellect

10

Trump was right

I don't know if it was John Stewart or the presidency of Barack Obama but I have been watching MSNBC for years. I mention John Stewart first because he's dope and because it was his satirical show on Comedy Central, which made politics palatable for me. I would hear the news from him and then watch the interviews he spoke about on their respective networks. I fell in love with MSNBC simply because of the way Steve Kornacki broke down the electoral map during election time. He was the first person to break the news that Barack Obama was going to win re-election and I've watched him break down those electoral maps ever since. However, if I were to become a political anchor I would be just like Ari Melber! He is intelligent, respectful and always has a hip-hop reference for you! On Fox News I enjoy Chris Wallace, which isn't hard for me considering the only Christopher I acknowledge, is Wallace (Biggie Smalls.) He is smart and follows the facts. On CNN I like Chris Cuomo and Anderson Cooper. But of all these contributors to political news Rachel Maddow is BAE (Bae is a term that can mean your significant other or someone you have great admiration for!) She has a masterful way of captivating me with her historical narratives. I never know how she will connect her introduction with the leading headline yet she never disappoints in doing so in a masterful way. I love how she shares information and the dignity she displays behind her desk. I love the fact that she shouts out her wife. I love her use of content and the fact that she will ask folk if she told the story right. I love me some Rachel Maddow!

2016 was a very crazy time for me. I honestly never thought Donald J Trump would be president. Between the things he did, said and all the allegations of sexual misconduct, I thought there was no chance he would win. Not to mention the fact that Hillary Clinton was the most over qualified candidate we ever had run for president. But he did! Since then I haven't stopped watching the news because there is always something going on. As destructive as Trump is, he is entertaining. And as I have watched MSNBC, CNN, and FOX, I can clearly see that Donald Trump is a liar. I mean it's easy to see. Anyone with hood knowledge can recognize a con man when they see him. Any person who uses hyperbole the way he does can't possibly be telling the truth. His phone calls are perfect, he is the only one who can save us, its because of him that we have a great economy, Mexico will pay for the wall.... blah blah blah. Miss me with all of that! From "it was locker room talk," to "I'm just trying to fight corruption," Donald Trump's lies a continuous and frequent. They also just so happen to be entertaining!

Despite that, there is a lot of truth to what Donald Trump says. This is important to say because if we disregard everything he says, we will miss out on issues that this country needs to address. One thing he said that was truthful is the fact that Adam Schiff mischaracterized his phone conversation with Ukraine. Schiff took great liberties with his creative interpretation. To do that is wrong and we should acknowledge that. There is a swamp that needs to be drained. There is way too much money in politics and as long as our politicians are serving two masters, it will be difficult for us to truly make meaningful progress in this country. There is so much money in politics that even the death of our children won't move politicians to reform gun laws. With companies contributing millions of dollars to political campaigns, politicians have the duel duty of satisfying their constituents and their donors. When they can only satisfy one they satisfy their donors and give us lip service. This goes for both the Democrats and Republicans. So in regards to the need for the swamp to be drained Trump was right.

Another thing Trump is right about is the fact that the media lies. Recently, I decided to watch more Fox News because I normally watch MSNBC. When you watch both networks you begin to realize that either one of them are lying or both of them are. If you watch Fox News, they will tell you that there is an all out attack on the President by the do nothing Democrats and the fake news. They will also tell you that there are spies and operatives lying on the President. They villianize the Democrats stating they are against the American people. Democrats on the other hand believe that the President is corrupt and needs to be out of office.

Whether it is the Whistle blower report or Donald Trump himself telling foreign countries to investigate the Bidens, Democrats villianize the President and this position is shared by MSNBC and CNN. Those positions skew how news is shared with viewers. Upon the release of the Mueller report MSNBC shared that it showed 10 areas where the President obstructed justice. Fox News stated it showed no collusion and no corruption. Fox News said it showed that the president didn't do anything wrong. One of these networks is lying to us. When the transcript was released Fox News said it showed that there was no quid pro quo (favor for a favor) between Trump and the leader of Ukraine. MSNBC stated it was clear quid pro quo. Both urged their viewers to read the document because his guilt or non-guilt was so apparent. I agree. We need to start reading things on our own because the media lies. Trump was right!

    In the beginning of his campaign run Trump made a bold came. Trump said he could walk down 5th Ave, shoot someone and people would still love him. I believe Trump was right when he said this. Donald Trump may not be shooting people on 5th Ave, but he is sho nuff killing this country. Trump was right about the swamp and the media so he uses part of that truth to manipulate his base to trust him. He says he is going to drain the swamp, and then swamps up Washington. He says the media *lies* and then demands that the media *lie* for him. He has created distrust for every system in this country. Since he didn't win the popular vote he creates a rumor that people illegally voted so we can doubt our voting system. A system that doesn't have an issue with voting fraud as it does voting attendance. We claim to be a country that values democracy but we don't even get a day off to vote. But I digress; after being told by his CIA and FBI that Russia meddled in our elections Trump has questioned their reliability. Trump even goes as far as asking other countries to investigate Americans. This is not to suggest things shouldn't be looked into. Hunter Biden was getting paid over $80,000 a month. That definitely sounds funny but America should be investigating him no one else. However, to sow distrust into our government intelligence community is also problematic. Trump speaks about the "Do nothing Democrats," who have passed tons of legislation waiting to be voted on in the Senate. This stokes the fire of partisan hatred in this country. When you state that certain politicians hate America and the American people because they oppose you, you are assassinating their character and making a narcissistic correlation between you and America. You are not America, Trump.

So, Trump has tried to kill our trust for the media, our intelligence community, politicians, and our newspapers. He even doctored a weather map and wanted us to trust him and not meteorologists that study weather. Trump is killing a lot of vital aspects of America that we will not be able to simply get back when he leaves. But again, Trump was right because people still love him. Despite the rape allegations, the vulgar language, the unkept promises, the tax cut for the rich, the multiple golf outings, exploitation of foreign officials and the like, Trump supporters still support him. That I honestly don't take issue with because anyone who voted for Trump knew who he was when they voted for him or at least they should have. I take issue with politicians who are cowering to Trump. I am not a Republican but I respect the republican ideology. I agree that there should be limited governmental control over individuals and states. I believe that we shouldn't have to pay high taxes. There are quite a few foundational republican beliefs I can agree with but the Republican politicians we have now are not fighting for those values. They are simply watching Trump kill this country and are doing nothing. To watch Trump kill this country while Republicans defend him is mind blogging. The same republican politicians who got on Obama for having a tan suit on and using a selfie stick defend Trump asking foreign countries to investigate our citizens. The same republican politicians who impeached Bill Clinton for lying to congress about his sexual impropriety sweeps away our sitting President's pay off to a Porn Star. While Trump is killing our global influence and American values republican lawmakers still love him at the cost of our country.

Donald Trump is an immoral, lying, con artist but he did reveal some truths about this country we need to be focused on after he is gone. We need to examine our media and demand objective truth. We need to question how our intelligence community handles American interests. We need to drain the political swamp that is not working for our people. Those things we must fight for regardless of who is in office. The most important thing we need to do is hold accountable all politicians who watched Trump tear down the foundations of this country and still loved him. That goes for Republicans who did nothing and Democrats who also did nothing. If you were on the wrong side of history, you should be held accountable. Donald Trump was wrong on a lot of things but I will be first to admit to you on some of topics Donald Trump was right!

The Completely Sporadic Thoughts of a Black Brooklyn Intellect

11

2 Different Leagues

Handball saved my life! Who would have thought gangstas and hustlers played handball? Well, they did. Playing handball in my teenage years introduced me to gang members in my neighborhood in a non-confrontational way. Because of this, I was cool with gangstas and hustlers of all sorts. They respected my game and I respected them. So, what started off as fear and concern ended with me having a family partly due to the fact that I played handball.

    Sports are a great galvanizer in the hood. When I was growing up, we played outside! And though handball was the sport I played the best as an older teen, I knew how to play all sports. When you went outside you didn't know what sport was going to be played but you were down to play. It could be basketball, football, baseball, tag, or kick ball; it didn't matter. You either knew how to play or were going to learn (especially if we didn't have enough people to play a game and someone was there. If they didn't know how to play they were gonna learn that day!)

We played sports in some of the worst conditions. We played football on concrete. We played basketball on slanted rims and cracked floors. The basketballs we played with had titties (bubbles on the basketball) on them so they bounced awkwardly. The handball court I learned how to play on was uneven with gravel all over it. But we played regardless of the dangers because of the "LOVE OF THE GAME!" If someone got injured during a game they were told to play through it. If you twisted your ankle, you simply tied your sneaker tighter. You got hit really hard; you were told to walk it off and man up! If you started bleeding, you would get a band-aid and keep on playing because you played for the "LOVE OF THE GAME!" Playing for the "LOVE OF THE GAME," is a phrase that signifies one's respect for the sport they are playing. It is a pledge of commitment of one's mind, body, and soul. It is physically paying homage to the legends that came before you in an effort to one day be a legend yourself. There was no money in it, just bragging rights and that was enough for most of us. And when you were really nice… when no one else could play a particular sport as well as you could, you could look at them and say, "You ain't even in my league! We in 2 different leagues!"

Playing sports is viewed as a way out the hood for some of us. Teens have dreams of making it to the league and becoming millionaires. They play for AAU teams then go to college and finally to the league. Through all this they are told to play for the "LOVE OF THE GAME!" Throughout this process their bodies are viewed as commodities. The talents of these athletes create revenue for colleges and the leagues in which they play. However, they are still told to play for the "LOVE OF THE GAME!" When they are injured they are still expected to play. When they lose loved ones or have family issues, they are still pressured to perform especially if their team needs them. When athletes enter free agency (this occurs when a player completes their contractual obligations to the team that they play for and is now looking for new employment) fans expect athletes to not simply play for the team that offers them the most money or even the best chance to win a championship, but to play for the "LOVE OF THE GAME" with little to no regard of those two factors. It doesn't matter if the team is horrible or if you will have to take a pay cut, athletes are conditioned and encouraged to play simply for the "LOVE OF THE GAME!"

Colleges, universities and Professional leagues do not function in this manner. I have learned through my 2 business degrees that the fundamental purpose behind any business is to create a profit. There is no *love* in business! League owners have a responsibility to their stakeholders to make money off of the sports business they run. Colleges raise tuition and gain revenue from playoff appearances, merchandise, TV deals, sponsorships and ticket sales. Colleges are able to build their names and gain revenue based on their sports programs. Student Athletes are not allowed to make money off of their talents and if they decide to go pro, they can never play college sports again. Student athletes receive scholarships and many other perks for playing a college sport. However, they don't get paid for their services. They are supposed to play for the "LOVE OF THE GAME!" The problem with this is, when an institution is functioning with the purpose of profit and the athletes are playing for the "LOVE OF THE GAME," they are playing in two different leagues.

I believe that folks go to college to increase their marketability in order that they can make more money. If one could get a high paying job without going to college, many wouldn't go. Student athletes must forfeit making revenue for themselves in order to go to college so colleges can make money off of them. Student athletes can't work, can't receive outside funds or go pro without penalty. However, the NCAA is a billion dollar institution. Coaches of many of the Division 1 NCAA teams make millions. These coaches are able to get sneakers deals not because of their own talent but because of the talent of their players. When schools make it to the playoffs they get bonuses yet the student athletes get none. They don't get paid because their scholarship is their payment. I think that is stupid. Student Athletes are in school so that one-day they could get paid. If their actions are generating income now, they should be paid now. No one should be able to profit off of the bodily efforts of someone else without paying them. If you have a billion-dollar institution there is no reason why student athletes can't get paid.

Once in the league, athletes have another issue. Owners are not obligated to win championships! Owners of business/teams are simply obligated to make a profit. Business is a matter of numbers not emotions. So, when players come into the league with a "LOVE OF THE GAME," mindset, they are at a disadvantage. Teams require a loyalty from players that they don't have to reciprocate. Case in point, Isaiah Thomas. Isaiah Thomas played for the Boston Celtics through injury and then lost of his sister. He played for the "LOVE OF THE GAME!" That off-season Isaiah Thomas was traded to the Cleveland Cavaliers for Kyrie Irving. Though he played for the love of the game, the business of the game took precedence. After being told he would not be traded, Demar Derozan was traded for Kahwi Leonard. Despite that fact that he was loyal to the Raptors, the business of the game took precedence. Players and owners are playing in two different leagues.

Even though this is the case, players are still told to play for the "LOVE OF THE GAME," and are criticized if they don't. When LeBron James took his talents to South Beach, people were upset. Likewise, when Kevin Durant went to the Golden State Warriors, fans were irate. However, these players were simply going to teams that would help them achieve their life long dream of winning a championship. If you had an opportunity to leave your job for a better one to achieve your dreams wouldn't you? If a company offered you millions of dollars to work and the team you worked with made your job easier, wouldn't you take the job? I believe we expect too much from athletes. If playing sports is a business, athletes should be able to treat it as such. They may love playing the game but they must always remember that it's a business. Dwayne Wade took a pay cut for LeBron James to be on his team and was promised he would be paid later. When it was time to get paid the team didn't want to pay him. There are players who stay loyal to teams and try to win championships the "right," way (this means hall of fame caliber players will stay on one team and wait for general managers to get the players they need) but this takes their dreams out of their hands. Additionally, if a team is making money via attendance and they are still losing (i.e. the Knicks) there is no incentive for the team to get better because it is still making a profit. Owners can understand that athletes have dreams of winning a championship but ultimately the business of the game is about making money.

I love sports! Sports saved my life! But I now understand that there can't be a "LOVE FOR THE GAME," unless both the athletes and the owners are operating with that purpose. If the game is about making a profit then athletes should function as such. If players want to win a championship, they should pursue that even if that means they are stacking a team (when all the good players all go on the same team). Athletes should be able to do what is best for them and their families without be criticized. As workers we make those types of decisions everyday. Colleges should pay student athletes. In fact all athletes who generate income should be able to receive compensation for their talents. There are

YouTube channels that chronicle high school players that generate income because of the skills displayed by the players but the players themselves can't get paid. This is exploitation and we need to make sure that student athletes are being compensated for the blood, sweat, and tears they shed for the game. Athletes are always one play away from being injured and never playing again. While institutions and owners have the option of getting another physical commodity to take their place. Athletes should be able to make as much money as they can while they can. If not we are exploiting them for loving the game.

    I know athletes get paid a lot of money and a chapter talking about how they should be getting more money seems strange. But I wanted to shed some light on the reality that players and owners play in two different leagues. Owners and institutions have one fundamental goal and that is profit. For athletes their hearts, souls, families, image, and dreams are tied up into the sport they love to play. If owners are able to function with profit being the bottom line, so should players. If players are obligated to play for the

"LOVE OF THE GAME," so should owners. If they don't, athletes are at a disadvantage. Students are going to continuously be exploited. So while you cheer for your favorite team, support the decisions of players who put their dreams and families first. I know they are supposed to play for the "LOVE OF THE GAME," but just know that the owners and them play in two different leagues!

12

The Working Man is a Sucka!

The Completely Sporadic Thoughts of a Black Brooklyn Intellect

I have been a big fan of Mobster movies ever since I was a teen. A close friend of mine and I would spend hours watching and analyzing the *Godfather* movies, *Casino*, *Goodfellas* and anything else mob related. My love for Godfather 2 is actually how I got my nickname Vito (that and the fact that people consistently mispronounce my first name). One particular mobster movie I personally love is the movie *A Bronx Tale*. *A Bronx Tale* isn't just your traditional mobster movie though. The movie deals with racism, interracial relationships and one's view of success. Oh and yea it has mobsters in it. The movie stars Robert Dinero, Chazz Palminteri (Sonny) and Lillo Brancato (Calogero) and is based loosely on the life of Dinero. Calogero's father who is played by Robert Dinero is a simple bus driver who works hard to provide a decent life for his family. Sonny is a well-known Mob boss who runs the neighborhood. All is well until Calogero witnesses Sonny beat someone up for a parking spot. When police come on the scene they questioned Calogero (they call him Cee in the movie so we will also, lol) about what he saw. Cee is asked to look at a line up which included Sonny and pick out who committed the assault. Though Cee was young, he seemingly understood the code of the streets that says, "you never talk to police," so when they asked him if he saw Sonny do it he said no. This eventually leads to Sonny taking Cee under his wing. Sonny gave Cee guidance on all sorts of things ranging from dealing with people who owed him money to dating. As Cee grew up he was able to see the difference between his father's lifestyle and Sonny's.

      Cee's father instilled values in him. He didn't want Cee to become a mobster so he worked hard to show him that there was nothing wrong with working hard for decent pay. There is pride in getting up every day and earning your money. That is how Dinero grew up and that was what he taught his son. In a contrast that mirrors Robert Kiyosaki's "Rich Dad, Poor Dad," (every child should read this book.) Sonny had a different perspective on success. Sonny believed "the working man is a sucka." The idea that someone would spend all day working for someone else made no sense to Sonny. Sonny was a hustler. Sonny was engaged in multiple endeavors that made him money (see I'm not a snitch either lol.) After a heated exchange between Sonny and Dinero, Dinero tells Cee that "its easy to pick up a gun but try getting up everyday! The working man is the tough guy!" To that I agree. However, I also feel Sonny has a point when he says the workingman is a sucka!

Growing up we are told to go to school and get good grades so we could go to college and get a good job. Once you get your job you are supposed to work for 20 to 40 years and then retire. I watched my mother and father do this. There were no conversations about passive or residual income. There were no conversations about multiple streams of income, unless it meant working multiple jobs. Basically I was raised (like many other people I know) to work for a living. This was and is tough. I've worked in customer service for 20 years and I've watched my mother as well as many other mother figures work their asses off. You have to be tough to be a worker.

During my teen years I fell in love with the concept of hustlin. Hustlin isn't just about selling drugs or doing illegal things; it's about finding creative ways to generate income. I fell in love with the concept because not only did working for 20 to 40 years seem daunting to me but also I realized that the current working structure is a rigged system. After working a few jobs, I quickly realized that working is more about who you know than what you know. Working hard isn't as important as who you slept with. The best workers are exploited for what they do and necessarily promoted. The blacker you are the harder it is for you to move up the ladder of success. And no matter how good your resume is, if you don't know the person receiving it, it's going to be hard to get a job. I have watched hardworking employees train their new bosses. I have watched qualified hardworking employees get passed over for positions based on their gender. Only to watch the company suffer from not promoting said employee.

      I have seen workers be loyal to their jobs only for their jobs to do them dirty. Asking for time off is never easy. Once you are sick or have an emergency you maybe fired. And the moment you become too much to pay, you are let go. We didn't even begin to talk about how toxic some of these working environments are. Many of my coworkers would come to work angry that they had to be there. They had big dreams of doing something else but society had tricked them into believing that there is long-term security in jobs and education. However, the recession of 2008 showed my generation that this wasn't the case.

The 2008 recession proved the working woman/man was a sucka. Many workers who did nothing wrong were let go because of greedy CEOs and executives. Students who graduated from school found that there were no jobs for them in their field and because they got their degree, they were overqualified for many of the jobs they had before they graduated. You compound that with the student loans they were required to pay back and you can see how many individuals felt suckered. All the while, companies and colleges still made money. Companies got bailouts and CEOs gave themselves golden parachutes (gave themselves large amounts of money before leaving the companies they messed up). For those who trusted in this structure of having one source of income, they were shit outta luck and had to find a way to survive. People worked multiple part time jobs to make ends meet. Folks who were able to keep their jobs had to do more work for the same pay. So even if you were able to work, you still were suckered.

Now let's pause for a second to talk about generational sucka advice. Now given the time period that *A Bronx Tale* was shot in, Dinero's advice to Cee wasn't really all that bad. He drove a bus, got paid a decent amount and was able to provide for his family. Many of our parents have taught us these principals based on how they grew up. The problem with that advice is that advice was temporal. These are very different times. So what was good advice 30 years ago is generational sucka advice now. In the 1980's before Regan privatized college education, students could pay for college by working summer jobs. Having a college education greatly increased your chances of employment as well as your potential pay when you finished school. It was also not uncommon to retire from your job after working 20-30 years. Therefore, telling your child to go to college, get a good job and stay there until they retired was solid advice. That is no longer the reality we live in. Going to college now is a financial investment that many students take years to pay back (if ever). People are literally getting rich off of the dreams of our youth. At this point, college degrees are like the high school degrees of the 80s, which means you are still in a large employment pool when you get your undergrad degree. In order to further distinguish yourself you need to get another degree, which requires more debt. Job turnover is extremely high so it is highly unlikely for a person to work 20-30 years at one job like it was back then. The advice given to us by our parents, though well intentioned, is outdated. The working woman/man is tough but they are also a sucka.

So what is the alternative? Not relying on a job for financial security! Be a hustla! As I worked I realized a few things;

1. I was smarter than a lot of my bosses in my 20's
2. It made no sense for me to work for someone who I was smarter than

3. If I was smarter than the boss why not work on being the boss someday and not the worker.

If I worked on being a boss I could hire who I wanted and build what I wanted. I could run my business how I wanted and I would be working for myself. I continued to get my education to open more doors. College is a lot more about networking than it is about education. Now my goal is to create multiple streams of income so if I lose one job I won't be in dire straits.

As a black man who watched his mother work hard to provide for me, I know that if I'm blessed to have children I want to provide for them just like my mom did for me. I just want to do it different. I want to set up my businesses (it's not that much to start an LLC which gives you all the tax breaks of a corporation so get on it) so I can be at home with my children. Writing this book is my attempt at creating passive income for myself (passive income is income that is continuously generated from you either doing something just once or by not doing anything at all.) 8 out of 10 Millionaires in 2014 made their money from real estate, so I plan on owning investment properties so other people can pay my mortgage. Also, I want to provide housing for black and brown folk as well as LGBTQIA+ teens who have been kicked out their homes.

If you write music you should own your publishing so you can license it out and get royalties from it (passive income.) There are tons of ways to make money without working under someone else who determines when you go on vacation or not. My ultimate goal is for my children to never have to write a resume in their lives. They will learn how to write one but I don't want their financial futures to be in anyone else's hands but their own. If I continue to network they will be able to get jobs by me making phone calls. If by businesses are successful I can hire them myself. By building a company and investing in real estate I can pass down assets to my kids and not debt. They will work but they will never have to succumb to this flawed working structure for them to be successful.

As black and brown people, we need to own our own (Random shout out to Killer Mike! Watch Trigger Warning!) We have the most talented basketball players in the world but don't own a lot of basketball teams. We created rap music but don't own our publishing. Our talent generates trillions of dollars yet it doesn't circulate into our communities because we don't own our own intellectual property. We have been conditioned as a whole to get up everyday and make someone else rich. Your rent helps to subsidize someone else's income. It's time for us to stop solely being the workers and to start being the owners/hustlas. We need to change the narrative we give our children and instead of giving them outdated well-intentioned generational sucka advice, give them assets that they can use to build an empire.

I stand on the shoulders of my ancestors whose hard work established the western hemisphere. I stand on the shoulders of my parents who worked hard for me to be where I am today. I will take that and work smarter so my kids will never have to work the way our ancestors worked. I'm going to work smarter because there is no security in a 9-5 but if I develop my mind to learn how to get passive income I can get money and raise my kids. No one should have a monopoly on your finances. So we as a community need to work on using our jobs to build our businesses instead of allowing our jobs to take away our dreams. Cee's father is right; to get up everyday and work for someone else is tough. But I believe Sonny is right as well, the workingman is a sucka!!

13

KANYE WEST IS A GENIUS!

The Completely Sporadic Thoughts of a Black Brooklyn Intellect

I would like to start off this chapter by saying that I don't agree with Kanye West's politics. I can understand that he is an independent thinker but I can't understand how he could support Donald Trump. When he recently said that Republicans freed the slaves (which is true by the way) I found it troubling because Republicans didn't agree to free the slaves because of their recognition of our humanity. Republicans didn't care about us and many of them still don't care about black people (the same can and should be said about Democrats.) It makes me cringe when I see him wear a maga hat. I also feel his comments at Howard University was absurd. To say "next time the slave nets come out, let's all try and not stand in one place," is disrespectful to our ancestors who fought for their freedom and decided to jump off the boat rather than become slaves. It shows his ignorance to our ancestors who were sold into slavery and others who were stolen in the middle of the night never to be seen again. And though I don't agree and are at times troubled by some of the things Kanye West says, I do respect his right to choose and support which ever political party he wants to support. Political Homogeny is not a prerequisite for me to enjoy Kanye's music. I can respectfully disagree with his politics and still respect him musically because regardless of who Kanye supports politically, Kanye West is a Fucking Genius!

    I had just clocked out to go on break from my job at Coldstone Creamery, on 42nd street, when I walked past a large crowd. The crowd was surrounding the MTV building that aired TRL (Total Request Live,), which was a show that would count down that day's top 10, requested videos. It was also a place where artists would go to debut new music videos or albums. While I walked past the crowd I saw Roc-a-fella signs and posters that had a teddy bear mascot on them. I had no idea what any of it meant but since I know my mans Hov was part of Roc-a-fella I was immediately intrigued. I saw that an artist named Kanye West had released an album that day so I went to the Virgin mega store that was across the street and bought the album.

The Completely Sporadic Thoughts of a Black Brooklyn Intellect

My boy and I had a ritual where we either listened to albums together or if we didn't, we would put each other on to an album we thought was dope. After I heard Kanye's first album I told my boy he had to listen to it. I never got my album back (Sherm I need that album back son lol.) That album "College Dropout," would sell 3 million copies and be widely considered a classic album. He followed that with his sophomore album "Late Registration," which was also considered a classic. On this album he introduced a new rapper who I consider the greatest lyricist of all times (no typo and @ me) Lupe Fiasco. What made these albums classic wasn't just the music; it was the subject matter. At a time where gangsta rap was the most popular form of hip-hop, Kanye West burst on the scene with 2 albums talking about the issues of black college students. Songs like "Slave Ship," were hymnals for students who had to do work-study while members of Black Letter Greek organizations could laugh at the Broke Phi Broke skits found on his second album. His first two albums were Pro Black and soulful. "All Fall Down," and "I'll fly away," are just two of the many songs that made you tap your feet while moving your soul! Kanye would go on to make more classic albums including "Graduation," "My Dark twisted fantasy," and "Life of Pablo," along with tons of songs, productions and features. Kanye's musical genius is undeniable.

      This genius did not come without hard work. Kanye said in his song Spaceships that he made 5 beats a day for 3 summers. So there is definitely hard work and commitment attached to his genius. But what really cemented in my mind that Kanye West is a genius was all the amazing stories told about him. Young Jeezy spoke about a time he sent Kanye a beat for him to rap on. Kanye changes the beat and writes to it but Jeezy can no longer use the song because the changes made it impossible for him to meet his album deadline. A few months later Kanye brings Jeezy to the studio to get his permission to use his adlibs on the song Jeezy originally gave to Kanye. Kanye told Jeezy it was a hit. That song was "Can't tell me nothing." Jeezy recalls a time they were overseas and were performing. When Kanye came out, he came out to that song and Jeezy saw 80,000 people sing along to a song that he originally gave to Kanye to rap on. Kanye West is a Genius.

Another story can be found on the Fade to Black DVD (Ralphy, I need my DVD back lol.) "Fade to Black," documented Jay-Z as he recorded what was supposed to be his last album. While watching the movie you see some of the greatest producers in the world pitch Jay-Z beats for his album "The Black Album." Timbaland played Jay-Z beats until Jay chose the one he wanted. That beat ended up being "Dirt off your Shoulder." Pharell made the beat for "Allure," (top 5 greatest Jay songs of all times) and compared it to Carlito's Way. Carlito's Way is a movie starring Al Pacino about a former gangsta trying to go straight. Pharell tells Jay that the beat represents if Carlito made it on the train (watch the movie to understand the reference). Jay-Z's response was, "That's your pitch?" But once the beat dropped it was undeniable. Kanye West on the other hand did something completely different than his talented counterparts. He pitched Jay-Z a vision. In the video you see Kanye tell Jay-Z, "this is the part where you get off stage and then the crowd starts yelling Hova, Hova, Hova, Hova..." I was shocked because I was at the concert yelling Hova and didn't realize that the idea came from Kanye. The video also shows Kanye pitching the bridge to the song Lucifer that Jay-Z also uses. Kanye West isn't just a rapper and producer he is also a visionary. Producing albums like "Be," by Common, "The Blueprint," by Jay-Z, introducing artists like Lupe, creating the Yeezy sneaker and being one of the dopest rappers of all time; Kanye West is indeed a genius. However none of these things exhibit the greatest proof that Kanye West is a genius. The greatest proof of Kanye West's genius is his unwavering belief in himself!

    Since the moment he was hired at Roc-a-fella records Kanye West told anyone who could listen that he was a rapper. Though others didn't believe him Kanye believed in himself. He didn't ask anyone's permission to be audacious nor did he dim his light because he was in a room with legends. He knew he was a legend before anyone else did. He didn't care if others believed in him because he believed in him. If you listen to artists that he has worked with for years, when interviewers ask them how has Kanye changed they say he hasn't. Kanye is still the same person he was when he first got signed. He also believed that this would happen. This audacious unwavering belief of self is what makes Kanye a genius. Imagine if we all had that audacity to believe in ourselves. Maybe just maybe the reason that you haven't reached your genius level isn't because you don't have it. What if your success is tied to you having a Kanye West genius level belief of self?

Jay-Z did not sign Kayne West at first. Dame Dash did. Jay also walked past J. Cole and didn't take his mixtape. Eminem gave Fat Joe 6 demos and Joe didn't listen to any of them. Jay-Z himself, was rejected from every record label before he decided to start his own. I'm saying all this to say, your unwavering belief of self has to be audacious. People will doubt you, discourage you and even look past you. This will include your family, close friends, teachers, Reverends, significant others and enemies. The most genius thing you can do in those moments is work hard to believe in yourself!

Some people won't believe it can be done until you do it so if you need them to believe in a vision God gave you; you may never make it. If you get nothing else from this book I pray that you understand how wonderfully and fearfully God made you! So forget all those who can't see it. Work your symbolic 5 beats a day for 3 summers and no matter who is in the room never forget who you are!

The most genius thing you can ever do is believe in yourself! That is what makes Kanye a genius and that can make you one also. I don't agree with Kayne's politics but that doesn't matter. What I have learned from Kanye is that no matter who else supports me, the most important support I can get (other than from God) is from myself! Believe in yourself even if no one else does because those may be the lives God has called you to change. Kanye West has done some dope things in his day. He has 21 awards, tons of platinum plaques, he was worked with some of the top artists in the industry and single handedly saved the "Adidas," franchise. Throughout all this, the greatest thing Kanye ever did was believe in himself and because of that I submit to you, that Kanye West is a genius!

14

Thank you

bell hooks

(All about Love)

I learned about love differently than other folk. My foundational understanding of love came from watching my mother take care of my father as he battled cancer. Not only did she care for him but she also had two more children so in the midst of her helping him with his battle, she conceived, carried and bore two additional children. Now if you add that number up with the two she had before, you are now looking at a strong black woman (remixed Jay's line, lol). For me, her strength looked like her going to work, taking care of my sister and I, going to the hospital for both my father's and her appointments, dealing with the relatives who frequented the house and then going to bed to do it all over again. My mother took care of my father until he passed away. During his last days he wouldn't eat from anyone else but her. So, my foundational understanding of love wasn't predicated on that warm and fuzzy feeling you get inside when you meet someone or based on sexual attraction. My understanding of love centered on nurturing, healing, caring, selflessness and sacrifice. This is something my mother did not just for my father but also for everyone in my house. So, when I thought about loving someone those were the first things I wanted to offer. Now because I never seriously thought about living past my teenage years I always yearned for a woman who could take care of my children if something happened to me. I mean I'm a black man in America. Most of my friends and families lived with single mothers. If I was going to have a wife I wanted her to be strong enough to provide for my kids if anything happened to me. Morbid, I know but that was (and to a certain point still is) a concern of mine. But the root of my understanding of love stems from watching my mom be strong and nurturing.

My dad was in and out of the hospital consistently after I turned 5, my father died when I was 8. He was a proud Garifuna man from Honduras. I am his namesake but as a child we were nothing alike. I don't know if it was by design but my father was my first rival. In the short time I had with my dad he inspired me to be a man like him while not wanting to be him. Like most boys growing up I knew then that my father is invincible. I have some of the greatest male mentors a man could have but flaws and all, my father is always number 1. Not even death could take that away from him. And that was who I wanted to be better than! My dad! So while I emulated him by watching baseball with him and all his other shows, I didn't root for his teams. One day we were watching a Yankees game and my father said that was his team. When the game was over I walked over to the tv to change the channel (children were the remotes back then) and I changed it to channel 9, where another baseball team was playing. I asked my father which team that was. He told me the Mets and I told him, "that's my team," and they have been ever since. My father and I would race to the store and bet on soccer games if the USA played Honduras. My father beat me in checkers all the time. He was my biggest competitor. And because of this, I gained a great sense of self from an early age. I wasn't simply Genciano's son, I was Genciano Clotter Jr. My father taught me to love myself at an early age and for that his invincibility lives through me. Thanks Dad!

As I got older my mom and I would talk about my father. My father was dope, but he did have his flaws. He was very patriarchal and believed in gender roles. However, he took pride in his role. My mom told me how when he got paid he would give her all his money and she gave him back what was left after the bills were paid. If my mother needed to go into my father's bank account and she asked him he got offended. He would question why she was even asking him. He'd simply say "just take the money." My father took his job as provider seriously and trusted my mom with the finances. Now I have business degrees so I handle my finances but I never had a problem sharing what I have with my significant other. I don't believe in gender roles like my father but I also show love by providing for people I care about. I show love for self by being able to take care of myself.

My father loved me and he loved my mom but the person I think he loved the most, was my older sister. My mother told me a story; my father got dressed to go out but my sister started crying. My mother told him to go to the party and she will be fine but he insisted that he would just put her to bed. Well he put both of them to bed, and he missed his party, new suit and all. She was his favorite but it worked, because I was his rival. We all felt loved and appreciated through the good times and bad. When my father passed away my mother and my older sister were the people I looked up to. Because she was older, I always wanted to be like my sister. That included playing double-dutch, playing hand games, and doing her homework (well she kinda suckered me into that.) That nurturing is why I want a daughter so badly. I have a theory. I think that father's can freely love their daughters in a way they are afraid to love their wives. Why? Your wife can leave you but your daughter is apart of you. It may not be true but it's a theory. I learned a lot about love from my family. Though the Disney movies looked good it didn't match my reality. Love is deeper than kissing someone for them to wake up. Love is deeper than sex. Love is deeper than aesthetics. Love is wiping your significant other's ass when they can't. Love is going to chemo and dealing with someone sick. Love can be really ugly. I learned about ugly love first and I thank God for it.

Growing up I learned about communal love. That was the love I received from friends and their families. I'm talking about the Haques, Caballaros, Harris/McNeils, St. Johns, Turner/Johnsons, Irvine/Thompsons and many more. When people think about the hood they think about the struggle and the struggle is real. What is also real, is the love. I always had a place to stay and a meal to eat because so many parents took me in. They treated me well and taught me vital life lessons. And my situation isn't an anomaly. Parents take other kids in all the time. Not necessarily as in adoption but just in regards to caring for them. If you lived in my building all the mothers were your mothers. I could knock on multiple doors and get a plate of food simply because they cared for all of us. Communal love is real in the hood. There is nothing quite like it.

As a teen, understanding what love is, was hard. I knew who I liked but most of the time it was aesthetic. What is funny about aesthetics when you are a teen is who you really like may not be who society says is attractive. There was a girl that I had a crush on, who was tomboy. She came to school on her birthday with a skirt on and I remember my friends whispering about how funny she looked. I thought she looked gorgeous, but was too much of a coward to say it. We actually met at a park one day and played basketball. It was one of the coolest most natural impromptu dates I ever had. We flirted but I never took the next step. The next week at school we said hi and nothing happened. Years later I kicked myself for not telling her how beautiful she was on her birthday and how attracted I was to her. Then, by chance I saw her on the train. At that point she was lesbian. Now I don't know if she was one the whole time or even if my words at the time would have made a difference but I told her how I felt back then when I saw her on the train. Not because I was trying to get with her but because it was true. We smiled and we laughed about it but I learned a valuable lesson from that experience. Love is audacious and has unique qualities. When you see something you like in someone, share it with them. It doesn't have to be sexual or even lead to something. Expressing love and sharing positive energy is an award in itself. My regrets in life seldom come from women I didn't sleep with or money I didn't make. My regrets stem from hurting others or not saying or doing something that would have helped someone. Love speaks with words, sign language, braille, and actions. Love Speaks!

My mother remarried and the guy she married hated us. Maybe he didn't hate us but it felt like it. To be honest I don't even know that he truly understands what love is. During my teen years there was a lot of yelling in my house. There were times where fists, spoons, chairs and other objects were thrown. From that I knew that I never wanted to be in a violent relationship or a relationship where yelling was normal. Girls I used to date would think I was crazy when disagreements got loud and I would calmly ask them if they wanted to just be friends. In those moments I realized that some of us have unhealthy ideas of what love is.

When violence, yelling, mistrust (yes that means looking through cellphones) and public outburst becomes commonplace in your relationship, something is wrong. This is not to suggest that your relationship is going to be perfect. All relationships are a work in progress. However, disagreements should be had with love and respect. Being mad doesn't give you the license to verbally or physically abuse someone you say you love (and that goes for both men, women and non-binary individuals.) When we stay in relationships that are unhealthy. That toxic environment becomes normalized. When the relationship finally ends and someone actually wants to love you, you end up bringing those toxic habits into the new relationship. So a huge part of love (especially loving yourself) is separating from unhealthy relationships. When you do, go to counseling and take some time to heal before getting into another relationship. Hurt people hurt people even if it's not on purpose. Love means protecting your peace and allowing yourself to heal.

Love is also realizing that every project isn't yours. One of the best gifts my ex girlfriend ever gave me (she gave me quite a few) is my "I MET GOD SHE'S BLACK," t-shirt. I wear it with pride and I also enjoy preaching in that shirt. I love the shirt because it challenges the misguided monolithic belief that God is male. Normalizing the male God belief is problematic because it reinforces patriarchy in the church and subjugates women in a matter that God never intended. I also loved the shirt because it's true. All the attributes that I've learned about God I have found in my mother(s) and adopted grandmothers. When I think about love, discipline, encouragement, nurturing, and empowerment I think of my mother. My mother is proof to me that God exists. Now, just because you have God in you doesn't mean you are supposed to be God. Do you know the serenity prayer? It's the prayer that goes:

God grant me the serenity (the state of being calm, peaceful, and untroubled) to accept the things I cannot change, the courage to change the things I can and the wisdom to know the difference.

Now, let's just focus on the first sentence. At my church, there are times that we as clergy get depressed. We preach and pastor in an effort to help and encourage people in the name of

Jesus Christ. We try our best to help as many people as we can because we believe we are called to do that. The issue is we are only called to help and save those that God has called us to. This causes a problem sometimes because there are times where we yearn to help those that God has called someone else to help. When our words can't fix the problem or we can't encourage someone to be better we either feel defeated or continue to commit ourselves to a mission (or project) not given to us by God. When you take on a project you weren't assigned (that God didn't give you) and commit to it, it becomes very unhealthy for you. So when we see our colleagues harming themselves in an effort to help others we ask them this question.

"Are you the lamb of God who takes away the sins of the world?"

The question is in reference to the bible verse John 1:29 when John the Baptist announces Jesus. It helps to remind us that we are called to help the cause of Christ not be Jesus. There are times were both men and women try to be Jesus in relationships when you aren't supposed to. There is nothing wrong with seeing potential in someone and wanting that to foster and grow. However, BABAAAY, Potential has a shelf life. Ladies please be advised that if you are looking for a project, turn your television to a DIY channel but if you want to be with someone make sure they are ready for you. There are some beautiful broken men (and women) out here that you are not called to fix. You are called to raise sons so they can learn from you and find another woman. If you decide to raise a man there is a possibility he will do the same thing. Men the same goes for you. Women (and men) are not damsels in distress waiting for someone to save them. They are highly capable individuals who should be working toward something. If they aren't doing anything with their lives don't try to be their motivation because if they already have you and are doing nothing, why would they ever need to change. Love is building with someone. When it becomes solely working on someone so they could be better, that could be problematic. Knowing the difference will save you time and heartbreak.

In seminary, a classmate of mine (Reverend David Malcolm McGruder look him up he is a BAD MAN!) gave me a book called *Will to Change* by bell hooks. I don't know why he gave it to me. He simply said the book was powerful and it made him think so he offered it to me with the mandate that I give it back (smart man.) So, I read the book and it changed my life. It opened my eyes to the toxic ways patriarchy harms men as well as women. When I was done with the book, I gave it back and I was hungry for more bell hooks. I saw that she had another book called, "All about Love," and I decided to read it. That book would forever change how I understood love. During a few of my past relationships, I would converse about the topic of love all the time with the women I dated. Books like the *5 love languages*, *All about Love*, and *The Bible* would cultivate many of my conversations with significant others who I wanted to grow in love with. When reading *All about Love* Hooks shakes your soul with bold words that hug you and strike you simultaneously. One quote that will forever stay with me is when she says:

The word love is used is such a sloppy way that it can mean almost nothing or absolutely everything

Hooks also calls for us to make our own workable definition of love. I did that. When I read books like *5 love languages* I evaluated which love languages I spoke as well as the person I was with. I forgot which love languages I received in the past but what I do remember was, I didn't get receiving gifts. What makes that important was one of my partners gave me gifts anyway. They gave some of the most thoughtful gifts I ever received. Receiving gifts then became my love language but I began to question why it wasn't before. Upon reflection I realized that after my father died many people who promised me gifts never kept their word to me. That disappointment hurt so much that I subconsciously decided that I would rather not get my hopes up than hope and be hurt. My negation of receiving gifts as a love language was predicated on a past hurt that I never healed from. By receiving love from someone else, I was able to learn a new love language. This showed me that love languages and transient.

As you continue to heal from past traumas and connect with people who love you romantically and platonically, your love language can change, Love is about healing and releasing. Love is more than just a feeling. Love is a verb.

    I hate being ignored or disregarded. There are many phrases for being ignored. Being left on read, curved, played etc. I know that I have value. When someone ignores me I feel they are devaluing me. When I continue to communicate with individuals that ignore me (boredom is the devil's playground) I have learned that I'm devaluing myself. Loneliness and boredom can make us do some unhealthy things. It will make us connect with people we know we have no business connecting with and dating below our purpose. Being loved and loving yourself will allow you to know when someone values you.

    I promised myself that I would always show love even when it got hard. The hardest time for me to show love is when I know someone is tryna play me. I'm also someone who doesn't believe that forgiveness means access. If I love you platonically or romantically and I feel that you played me, we will not have the same relationship we had in the past. My forgiveness allows for the possibility of a new friendship but never what was once had. Love is about being considerate of other people. The funny thing about curving people is its universal. Phrases like, I'll get back to you, I'll let you know, oh I wasn't by my phone or if I don't have anything else to do, I'll let you know is OD disrespectful. An answer that can leave both parties with value and respect is simply "NO." As a young teen and even in my twenties I would entertain such phrases but as I got older I realized that people will only treat you how you allow them to treat you. Even well intentioned people can subconsciously take you for granted if you are not careful about your worth. Loving myself means I don't allow people to just treat me any kind of way. That also means I don't ignore or disregard other people as well. Love is accountability to you and to others. Love yourself enough so even when you are bored and lonely you don't do self-destructive things with toxic people. I know it may not be easy but you're worth it.

The Completely Sporadic Thoughts of a Black Brooklyn Intellect

I learned love from my parents, my community and my church. My church allowed me to love as a grown man. I'm able to love like my 7-year-old self. Now that can be problematic for a society that isn't used to a 6'1' black man platonically showing love in a non patriarchal sort of way. It's easy to misinterpret my showing love for me having an ulterior motive or me having an attraction to you. It's funny how love is so needed in this world but when you show love you are either rejected or exploited. I love my church so much because it not only created a safe place for me to show love but it is also a place where I continuously receive love as well. So, I show love with my whole heart and spread it (Spread love it's the Brooklyn way – Biggie.)

I have hopes for finding romantic love without obsessing over it. I nurture, encourage and empower people around me while being mindful to do it for myself. I hold my friends accountable to being their best selves and called them out, when they ain't shit. Love is accountability. I fight for the people I love (yes these hands work) because love always protects. I use love to embolden myself to do the things I'm scared to do because I believe God is love and love is the most revolutionary power in the universe.

You can find love in food through communion. Love is salvation. When I was lost in patriarchy, I found the will to change. Without your books I wouldn't be able to love the way I do and I hope my book helps others the way you helped me. I love you and this final chapter was all about love. Thank you, bell hooks!

The Completely Sporadic Thoughts of a Black Brooklyn Intellect

www.ingramcontent.com/pod-product-compliance
Lightning Source LLC
Chambersburg PA
CBHW031115080526
44587CB00011B/975